EVERYMAN,
I WILL GO WITH THEE
AND BE THY GUIDE,
IN THY MOST NEED
TO GO BY THY SIDE

EVERYMAN'S LIBRARY
POCKET POETS

UYGHUR POEMS

●●●●●●●●●●●●●●●●●

EDITED BY
AZIZ ISA ELKUN

TRANSLATED BY
AZIZ ISA ELKUN
AND OTHERS

EVERYMAN'S LIBRARY
POCKET POETS

Alfred A. Knopf   New York   London   Toronto

THIS IS A BORZOI BOOK
PUBLISHED BY ALFRED A. KNOPF

This selection by Aziz Isa Elkun first published in
Everyman's Library, 2023
Copyright © 2023 by Everyman's Library
Translations by Aziz Isa Elkun copyright © 2023 by Aziz Isa Elkun
Copyright information for other translators can be found in the
Acknowledgments section at the back of this volume.

everymanslibrary.com
www.everymanslibrary.co.uk

ISBN 978-1-101-90834-1 (US)
978-1-84159-830-7 (UK)

A CIP catalogue record for this book is available
from the British Library

Typography by Peter B. Willberg

Typeset in the UK by Input Data Services Ltd, Bridgwater, Somerset

Printed and bound in Germany
by GGP Media GmbH, Pössneck

CONTENTS

MODERN POEMS *(1900 to 1960)*

CONTEMPORARY POEMS *(1960 to 2022)*

FOREWORD

Uyghur poetry is rich and colourful; it reflects the magnificent natural landscape of Central Asia, with its endless steppes, soaring mountain ranges and mysterious deserts where the Uyghurs have lived for the last two millennia at the heart of the famous Silk Road. The frequent political turmoil, oppression, and wars that the Uyghurs have endured over the centuries as they fell under the rule of ruthless empires or were caught up in the feuds of local warlords, have all left their mark on Uyghur poetry, which is typically focused on migration and exile, war and peace, as well as universal themes of nature and love. Uyghur poetry is diverse and multifaceted because it mirrors the complexity of the history of the Uyghur and their shifting politics.

The Uyghurs and their poetry are still too little known to English-speaking audiences. Before I focus on Uyghur poetry, let me briefly explain who the Uyghurs are. The Uyghurs are a Turkic people, and their name appears in the historical records around the second century CE. The word Uyghur means 'Union' or 'Federation'. In ancient times, Uyghurs lived in what are today the south-west Mongolian steppelands which adjoin the Altay and Heavenly Mountains (Tengritagh) and stretch further south to the oases of the Taklimakan desert and the Turpan Basin. These are largely the lands they continue to inhabit today. In their commonly shared cultural geography, the Uyghurs are one of Central Asia's earliest settled Turkic peoples.

11

The Uyghurs have followed many different religions, including Tengrism (sky worship), Shamanism and Manichaeism, Nestorian Christianity and Buddhism. From the tenth century onwards, they began to adopt Islam, which remains the predominant religion today.

In the mid-eighteenth century their last independent rulers, the Khojas, were overthrown by the Chinese Qing dynasty as it expanded into Central Asia. In the nineteenth century the Chinese government officially named the Uyghur homeland 'Xinjiang', which means 'new frontier' in Chinese. Uyghurs prefer to call their homeland East Turkistan or Uyghuristan. After the collapse of the Manchu Chinese Empire in 1911 the Uyghurs twice established short-lived independent states, once in 1933 and again in 1944. The latter ended in October 1949 when the Chinese Red Army occupied the region – with some military assistance from the Soviet Union – and it was incorporated into the People's Republic of China. Today, according to the Chinese government census, twelve million Uyghurs live in East Turkistan. Over two million Uyghurs live in the Central Asian states and in smaller diaspora communities across the Middle East, Europe and North America.

Throughout history, poetry has reflected human life in all its aspects and given voice to every human emotion. Transmitted from generation to generation both orally and through the written word, it has arrived in the present day in many different forms. Uyghur poetry has not developed in isolation. The Uyghurs lived on the famous Silk Road, and for many centuries they dominated the trade caravans that traversed the region. When camel trains crossed the deserts and passed through the mountains with goods from the Tang capital of Chang'an or from Constantinople in the Eastern Roman Empire, the sound of their bells carried echoes of far-flung civilizations beyond the horizons of the steppe. These geographies and histories underpin the character of Uyghur poetry, which demonstrates a dynamic capability to observe and adapt the new ideas and cultural influences which travelled along the Silk Road before the sea routes opened.

The Uyghur language belongs to the Qarluq branch (also known as Chagatay) of the Turkic languages of the Ural-Altaic family. It is closely related to the languages spoken by Turkic people from Central Asia to the Anatolian plateau. We can trace the written record of Uyghur poetry back to the first Uyghur script which was created and widely adopted in the sixth century. In this period, the Uyghur language became the primary literary language of many Turkic-speaking peoples.

The ancient oral traditions of Uyghur poetry provide the foundation of modern Uyghur language and literature. Among Turkic peoples, the oral epic poem is a widespread phenomenon. Tales of kings, saints and heroes, wars, pilgrimages and miracles were told by bards in the marketplace and at holy shrines or sung by musicians at social gatherings. Enriched with each retelling, these tales were passed from generation to generation, and they have played a hugely significant role in transmitting Uyghur history. An important example of this genre is the 'Epic of Oghuzname'. One of the earliest Uyghur poems, it is thought to have originated in the second century BCE, and was shared by the Uyghurs and other Turkic peoples. In the tenth century CE, this epic was recorded in the Uyghur script. Alongside the accounts of heroic acts and battles, the theme of love is prominent, as this extract shows:

> She was so beautiful that
> If she smiled, Heaven also smiled
> If she cried, Heaven also cried
> When Oghuz Khan saw her
> His whole body started to tremble
> He fell unconscious
> He fell in love and married her . . .

In later centuries, Uyghurs continued to compose poems in order to spread news, record significant contemporary events or the tragedies of war, and to keep recent history alive in the collective memory. Public transmission of such verses was essential, and again, they would often be set to music and sung in the bazaar. Here are some stanzas from an anonymous ballad lamenting the death of the nineteenth-century ruler Yaqub Beg:

> Yaqub Beg was a great man,
> He became King of the Six Cities.
> When they heard of Yaqub Beg's death,
> The Tungans arrived in Aqsu.

The Chinese arrived from Beijing,
Showing their fake smiles.
Our lords and officials ran away,
Showing their tails behind.

The angels in the sky
Wore fairy robes.
Ladies, do not shed your tears,
Yaqub Beg lives in heaven.

The written tradition of Uyghur poetry dates from the ninth century when poems on religious and philosophical subjects were composed at the courts of the Idiqut Uyghur Khanate, a practice which continued under the Uyghur Qarakhanid Kingdom in the city of Kashgar, and right up to the sixteenth century in Yarkand, the capital city of the Saidiye Uyghur Kingdom. In the earliest surviving examples we can see the influence of different belief systems. During the long era of Tengrism and Shamanic belief, prominent tropes and symbols included the power of the sky and the sun, a mysterious beautiful woman or a lone wolf encountering a hero in the forest. These ancient symbols still reverberate in modern Uyghur poetry. Poetic fragments from the Manichaean and Buddhist eras explore human spirituality, the world and the afterlife, the belief in reincarnation and the role of meditation as the means to reach Nirvana:

From the beginning of time, desire and vanity
have existed together, intertwined, one enemy.

A bitter, loveless heart is a poisonous snake.
But if one can live in an avaricious world free of
   greed,
in a discordant society uninfected by discord,
standing firmly on the earth, one will reach the
   unblemished
pure land and in an instant realize the body of a
   moral king.

When the Uyghurs began to embrace Islam in the tenth century, the new religion brought ground-breaking changes, transforming social and cultural life. The practice of writing poetry became more widespread thanks to the Islamic emphasis on literacy and learning. The eleventh-century scholar Mahmud Kashgari made the first written record of Uyghur folk poetry which had been transmitting orally for centuries. His *Lughat* provides an invaluable literary resource. Here is a quatrain teaching the importance of hospitality towards guests, for which Uyghurs are well known:

> When a guest arrives, help him dismount
> Make him feel at home and at ease
> Mix barley and hay for his horse
> And brush its coat to sleekness

Over time Uyghur poetry absorbed significant influence from the Persian and Arabic poetic traditions, as these languages, along with the Arabic script, came to dominate literary culture across Central Asia.

Traditional free verse and simple rhyme-based poetry continued side by side with new and more complex verse forms, which in pattern and variety closely followed Middle Eastern models.

During the thirteenth and fourteenth centuries, Uyghur poetry underwent a further change, embracing the Sufi poetic tradition which first flourished in the Arabo-Persian sphere before being adapted to the Turkic languages. This shift was cemented in the contributions of the great Central Asian poet Ali-Shir Nava'i of Herat (1441–1501). His extraordinary poetry and other literary work successfully established Turkic Chagatay as a literary language able to communicate profound emotion and beauty. Uyghurs recognize Nava'i as central to their literary heritage, regarding the poet as being of Uyghur descent. They continue to share and circulate his poetry, not only in written form but also singing it in Sufi gatherings and musical performances.

> I grieved after I saw your beauty for the first
>   time,
> And wished to see your alluring eyes for a
>   second time.
>
> Ready to strike with a knife to see you for the
>   third time,
> I will see on her face a beautiful mole on the
>   fourth time we meet.
>
> I will martyr myself for love on the fifth look,

I wish to meet you and see your beautiful eyes for
   a sixth time.

No other beauty like you exists in the seven
   continents,
You are beautiful like a fairy, and I wish to fly
   over you eight times . . .

This is part of a ghazal, the most common verse form
in the Uyghur Sufi tradition along with quantitative
metres (*arūz*). Both are derived from classical Arabic
and Persian poetry. A ghazal usually consists of around
twenty or more syllables per line arranged in fixed
rhythmic patterns, and its length varies from two to
twenty lines or more. Ghazals have many rhythmic
metres, and are rather more sophisticated than the con-
ventional quatrains used in earlier Uyghur poetry. The
ghazal is a beautiful poetic genre that fully expresses
the poet's emotions, infatuation with beauty, the
unbearable pain of loss and the sorrow of separation
from divine love. Another poet whose work is largely
in ghazal form is the wandering dervish Baba Rahim
Mashrab. The tales of his travels across Central Asia
still inspire Uyghur audiences today, and his passionate
mystical poetry forms an important part of the lyrics
of the large-scale Uyghur classical music suites – the
Twelve Muqam.

Madness has come over me, and love's fire is
   burning,
If I devote myself to this, will anyone visit me?

I have no patience left to stay, and I cannot leave,
With this fierce fire burning in my heart, will
   anyone visit me? . . .

No one knows how much poor Mashrab has
   suffered,
If I leave this place, will anyone visit me?

This selection includes a number of poems by Zahir-ud-Din Muhammad Babur (1483–1530), the founder of the Mughal Empire of India. He was born and grew up in Central Asia, and his mother, Kutluk Nigar, was a member of the family that would establish the Yarkand Uyghur Kingdom in 1514. Babur was strongly influenced by Ali-Shir Nava'i's ghazal lyrics, but also wrote poetry in the rubaiyat style — that is, in quatrains. Many of his poems derive from personal experience, describing the suffering and homesickness of a man who spent much of his life in exile. Even his Indian conquests brought him little joy.

Though you have given me fortitude through
   love
You have also condemned me to the pain of
   separation.
I implore you, make me as powerful as Nava'i
As though you were contacting a man already
   dead.

And again:

I have suffered agonies because of my cursed fate
I have done all I can, but it has ended in
    transgression.
I am facing the dilemma of India, and must
    abandon that tired place
Despite all of this, great God, please do not take
    away my good fate.

The metrical styles perfected in the classical era continued to shape the development of Uyghur poetry for centuries, and are still influential today. However, during the last decades of the twentieth century exposure to Russian poetry in particular brought new influences to bear – modernism, post-modernism and free verse have all had their impact. Take this example of 'hazy' (*gungga*) poetry by Ekhmetjan Osman:

Drum Dance

The wind of revelation
casts God to the dirt
when the call to prayer sounds in the body
    mosque

Clay Oven

The wine chased out of the city
blooms in gold –
it is the mind we have forgotten.

In the twenty-first century, the increasingly repressive policies of the Chinese government have included tightening restrictions on the use of the Uyghur language. In recent years the government has used full-scale force to assimilate the Uyghurs into Han Chinese culture. In this devastating period, when over two million people, including many writers and poets, have been detained in Chinese internment camps, Uyghur poetry has become a key weapon in the fight for justice and freedom, and for the survival of Uyghur language and culture. Poets have reflected on the ongoing tragedy in their homeland and the trauma and sufferings of the exiled Uyghur community, creating a new genre of Uyghur Genocide literature. Every Uyghur in exile today can tell a similar story of lost and vanished friends and family members. In this period we have also seen the rise of a new generation of outstanding Uyghur women poets. Here is Gülnisa Imin Gülkhan:

> They don't want to shed their tears
> They just want to lift their heads
> They just want to gaze at the sunless sky.
> Their troubles, their yearning
> Their nightmares and sleepless nights
> They want to talk about it with someone on the
>   outside.

I have contributed my own voice to remembering the Uyghur poets who have been imprisoned for their writing:

I want to break this iron cage
I want to break the world's silence
I want to fly
Free as a bird in the blue sky.

I have also translated the poems of imprisoned poets in order to introduce their excellent work to the world and to raise awareness of their situation. Here are some lines from the well-known Uyghur poet Adil Tunyaz, who was arrested with his whole family in 2017:

The homeless birds
Cry for the seasons, calling for their homeland
While the wandering wind carries
Leaves of its own.

He and others like him refuse to be silent in the face of exploitation, persecution and genocide, and their poetic voices both move and challenge. Imprisoned poet Perhat Tursun writes:

Let's not blame life for being meaningless
One day loneliness will reach its peak . . .

Let's cry, maybe our tears will be beautiful
If they are shed silently for love . . .

Let's not seek beauty only in the rose
The trace of blood on the thorn has beauty as
    well . . .

This is the first published English-language anthology to attempt an overview of Uyghur poetry, encompassing both its historical development and contemporary situation. Due to language and cultural barriers, and the dearth of Uyghur poems already translated into English, the project proved far more time-consuming than expected. Despite this, given the extraordinary political pressures and the urgent need to promote Uyghur culture on the international stage, I have worked hard to complete the book, which includes many poems that I have translated myself, as well as other poetry translators' valuable work. Though I am a poet, translator, and native Uyghur speaker, I faced challenges in translating from my native tongue into English, and I am grateful to my wife, Rachel Harris, who worked with me on many of the translations. Finally, here is one of my poems dedicated to my beloved mother, with whom I lost contact in 2017. My greatest hope is that she is alive and well.

The place where I was born
Has turned into a heap of ghostly relics
It exists only as a memory . . .

My roses are blossoming with hope
Singing a song of freedom
Without waiting for the spring
They remind us
How beautiful it is to be alive
To live in peace in our beautiful world.

I hope you will enjoy reading this collection of Uyghur poetry, and I ask you not to forget the Uyghurs and their poetic voices which speak out for humanity, love, freedom and justice. Thank you.

Aziz Isa Elkun
London, 2023

CLASSIC POEMS

ALP ER TUNGA*
Uyghur epic from Diwan-i Lughat al-Turk

Has Alp Er Tunga died?
Has he left this evil world behind?
Has fate taken its revenge?
Now our hearts are torn apart.

Men are howling like wolves,
They shout and tear at their collars,
They scream with all their might,
Their eyes rolling with grief.

The age was waiting for this moment,
The thief has set his trap,
The lords deceive each other.
Even if we flee there is no escape.

One can get used to anything,
There are many reasons to carry on,
But when the arrows of the age target them
Even the mountain tops are crushed.

The lords have exhausted their horses.
Grief has made them rise up,
Their cheeks and faces are pale,
Yellow like the saffron crocus.

The torches have been extinguished
And removed from the palace.
It was ordered
As soon as the fatal arrow killed him.

If the age shoots its arrow at such close range,
Who will save Turan?†
Not only will the mountains be hit,
But the valleys also will be torn apart.

* Alp Er Tunga is a mythical hero who may have been based on
a historical figure from the sixth or fifth century BCE. 'Alp' is
an old Turkic word meaning 'warrior', 'Er' means 'a man' and
'Tunga' is 'tiger'. Alp Er Tunga was a symbol of extraordinary
bravery. He marched against the Persians and the Arabs. He
tackled wild beasts and once captured a tiger. He also appears
in the Persian epic, the *Shahname*, as King Afrasiab. Alp Er
Tunga was eventually defeated by the Persians and killed by
trickery. The poem telling of his deeds is believed to be one
of the oldest epics of the Uyghurs and other Turkic tribes. It
was first written down in Mahmud Kashgari's *Diwan-i Lughat
al-Turk* in eleventh-century Kashgar during the Qarakhanid
dynasty. In the same period Alp Er Tunga also makes an
appearance in Yusuf Has Hajib Balasaghuni's *Kutadgu Bilig.*

† Turan is the Persian name for a region in Central Asia,
literally meaning 'the land of the Tur'.

MAHMUD KASHGARI (1005–1102)
TRANSLATED BY AZIZ ISA ELKUN

OGHUZNAME EPIC*

Under the sky of brightness
A girl was sitting alone
She was as beautiful as a fairy
On her forehead a shining mole
Glowed like an ember
Gleamed like an iron nail.

She was so beautiful that
If she smiled, Heaven also smiled
If she cried, Heaven also cried
When Oghuz Khan saw her
His whole body started to tremble
He fell unconscious
He fell in love and married her . . .

'I have become your King
Take up your bows and shields
Godly power should be our mark
The grey wolf will be our battle spirit.

'Our iron spears will be a forest
Livestock will roam on the hunting ground
Let the rivers and streams flow
The Sun will be our flag
and the Sky will be our tent.

'I am King of the Uyghurs
When I call, those who answer
Will be rewarded
And I will become their friend.

'Against those who do not answer
I will march in rage with my soldiers
I will make them my enemy.

'My sons,
I have lived long
I have been through many battles
I have shot many arrows from my bow
I have ridden many roads on my stallion
I have made my enemies suffer and cry
I have brought my friends joy
I have fulfilled my debt to Heaven
Now I bestow my land on you.'

* *Oghuzname* is an oral epic (*dastan*) telling of the legendary
ruler Oghuz Khan, which has its roots in the second century
BCE. It was transmitted orally for over a thousand years
among the Turkic-speaking peoples of Southern Siberia, the
Mongolian steppe, and Inner and Central Asia. The first
manuscript version of the epic was written in the old Uyghur
script in the thirteenth century and is preserved in the
Bibliothèque Nationale de France in Paris (MS Supplément
turc 1001).

THREE POETRY FRAGMENTS
UNEARTHED AT TURPAN BEZEKLIK*

From the beginning of time, desire and vanity
have existed together, intertwined, one enemy.
A bitter, loveless heart is a poisonous snake.
But if one can live in an avaricious world free of greed,
in a discordant society uninfected by discord,
standing firmly on the earth, one will reach the
    unblemished
pure land and in an instant realize the body of a moral
    king.

Fragment 1: 80 T.B. 1,598

One who worships Buddha embraces the seven
    treasures:
Their merits and good deeds will be measurable.
But one who worships and respects this Sutra:
Their merits and good deeds will be immeasurable.

Fragment 2: 80 T.B. 1,596-1

What knowledge you seek, learn on your way.
Think more, grow in self-awareness, do not boast.
Of that which you engage in, be vigilant and steady.
That is how you will shine bright above others.

I read this with hopeful eyes and send it to you.

Fragment 3: 80 T.B. 1,522

* The Turpan settlement, strategically placed on the Silk Road, was noted for its Buddhist culture from around the fourth century until it was fully Islamized in the fifteenth century. The remarkable Bezeklik Buddhist caves, about forty-six kilometres north-east of modern Turpan, are evidence of the area's importance as a religious centre. Turpan was the capital city of the Idiqut Uyghur Empire in the ninth century. The territory ruled by the Uyghurs varied over time, but Turpan and its immediate environs remained of political and cultural significance until the thirteenth century. These three fragments date from the eighth to the eleventh centuries.

QUATRAINS FROM *DIWAN-I LUGHAT AL-TURK* *

ON GUESTS

Dress yourself in a beautiful robe
Offer delicious food to your guest
Treat your visitor with respect
And your good name will spread

*

When a guest arrives, help him dismount
Make him feel at home and at ease
Mix barley and hay for his horse
And brush its coat to sleekness

ON FESTIVALS

Let us drink thirty glasses and sing
Then let us stand up and dance
To leap as a lion, roll and roar,
With cheers, chase sadness away

*

Let the young ones do the work
Shake fruit from the trees
Hunt wild horses and deer
For the festival, while we drink

* The poems from Mahmud Kashgari's *Diwan-i Lughat al-Turk*
(Dictionary of the Turkic Languages), 1074, give readers some
sense of the long tradition of Uyghur folk poetry stretching
back into the distant past. Songs and poems were often
composed in rhymed quatrains. There are thousands of them in
Kashgari's book and other medieval texts from Turpan.

MAHMUD KASHGARI (1005–1102)   33
TRANS. DOLKUN KAMBERI AND JEFFREY YANG

ON KNOWLEDGE
From *Kutadgu Bilig**

Gold is only ore beneath russet earth
Unearthed it becomes the ornament of a crown.
If a scholar doesn't impart his knowledge
His wisdom, hidden for years, sheds no light.

*

If there are no scholars, no wise ones,
Even grain will not grow from tilled land.
Their knowledge is a light for us humans,
If bright enough, it will dispel the darkness.

* Knowledge Leads to Happiness. The *Kutadgu Bilig* is a
Turkic 'mirror for princes', a wide-ranging text advising rulers
on how best to rule, teaching moral values, and discussing
many aspects of contemporary life and thought. Great
emphasis was put on education in medieval Islamic society.
Uyghurs valued the acquisition of knowledge and scholars were
highly respected, hence the blossoming of Uyghur literature in
this period.

YUSUF HAS HAJIB BALASAGHUNI (*c.*1019−85)
TRANSLATED BY DOLKUN KAMBERI
AND JEFFREY YANG

WISDOM OF ROYAL GLORY (1)
Excerpts from *Kutadgu Bilig*

This world is like a colorful shadow.
If you try to chase it, it will run away.
If you run away, it will chase you.

However much wisdom you possess,
seek more, for the wise man attains his desire by
    inquiry.

There are many differences among men,
but the main source of inequality is the degree of
    wisdom.

Wisdom is a type of wealth that cannot turn to
    poverty
and cannot fall victim to theft or fraud.

Man's heart is like a bottomless sea
and wisdom is the pearl that lies in its depths.
But if man fails to bring the pearl out of the sea
it might just as well be pebble.

Intellect and wisdom are great things;
if you find them, use them and fly to the sky.

Not a trace of fist or sword will remain,
man will die and only his words will remain.

Oppression is like a raging fire, it burns anyone who
    gets close;
justice is like water and extinguishes that fire.

The intellect's ornament is the tongue and the
      tongue's ornament is the word;
man's ornament is his face and the face's ornaments
      are the eyes.

YUSUF HAS HAJIB BALASAGHUNI (*c.*1019–85)
TRANSLATED BY AJINUR SETIWALDI

WISDOM OF ROYAL GLORY (2)
Excerpts from *Kutadgu Bilig*

Ch. V
Know that three are spring stars and three summer,
three autumn, and three winter.

Three are fire and three water, three wind,
and three earth. . . .

God who brings order from chaos himself arranged
it thus, bringing peace and order among them.

Ch. XLIV
He made the sun to shed light upon this dark domed
house of clay.

He brought into being the blue sky, raising it aloft,
and adorning it with sun and moon and stars.

Below, brown earth and blue water; above, pure air
and fire.

Hot and cold, dry and moist: these did He bring into
harmony and apportion to His creatures.

Ch. LXV
Adam's son, if he claims to be human, should be able
to distinguish hot and cold.

He must understand the body's natural constitution,
eat what agrees with it and refrain from what does
    not. . . .

Hearken to the words of the physician, my lamb:

The bodily humors I recount; red blood, white phlegm, yellow bile, and black.

They are enemies each to each: when one advances drive it back.

In order to keep one's natural humors in balance one must eat only what agrees, and this requires the exercise of intellect.

This, my son, is what distinguishes man from beast.

So heed these words of the wise greybeard, and do not remain a savage:

If a man reaches forty and does not know his own natural humor, then he is wholly a beast, albeit he may speak.

Ch. LXXVII
Many dreams come according to what one eats and drinks. If you eat something that disagrees with you, you will have a disagreeable dream.

Others come according to the season of the year, and which of the humors is predominant.

If it is spring, and a very young man sees in his dream all red things and the brown earth,

It is a sure sign that the sanguinary humor is predominant, and he needs to be bled.
If it is summer, and a young man dreams of yellow and orange, or of saffron and ground corn,

Then the yellow bile is predominant and he should be given Persian manna as a purgative.

If a mature man, in autumn, sees a black mountain, or a well, or any hole,

Then the black bile is predominant and he should be administered a potion that will clear his brain.

And if an old man, in winter, dreams of running water or of ice and snow and hail,

Then his phlegm is predominant and he should be given hot food and drink as remedy.

HIKMET (1)*

Of those who enter this life, none can avoid death
People living in this world never value each other.

There is no escaping from mourning in this world
If you understand this, then do not attach yourself to
    the world, for it is faithless.

Look down beneath your shoes to where you will lie
    alone in the dust
You never imagine yourself in such a position.

But you will lie in the grave not knowing whether it is
    summer or winter
Your son, daughter and friends cannot look after you
    then.

After your death, your children will take away your
    wealth
Nobody will know how you pass your time
    underground.

In this brief life there is no need for a destination
People who think of death should give no passion to
    this life.

Those who think of hell fire and torment in the grave
Will not be at ease until they have crossed the bridge
    to Paradise.

Those who come to the afterlife with faith
Listen to them in that place, but you cannot die with
    them.

* Hikmet (wisdom) verses, like these attributed to Yasawi,
still circulate in the oral tradition today. They are recited by
rural religious specialists in their rituals, and preserved in
handwritten notes.

KHOJA AHMED YASAWI (*fl.* 12TH CENTURY)
TRANSLATED BY AZIZ ISA ELKUN
AND RACHEL HARRIS

HIKMET (2)

It will dry the saliva in your mouth
Extinguish the light in your eyes
You will enter into the dust
Be fearful of death.

Awake Khoja Ahmed, slave of God
These words are no lies
You will be left in the dust
Be fearful of death.

Palaces will be destroyed
Orchards moved away
It is the same for us all
Death will come, will it not?

Wives will be widows
Gardens will be abandoned
Orphans will weep
Death will come, will it not?

Awake, Sulayman
These words are no lies
You will be left in the dust
Be fearful of death.

KHOJA AHMED YASAWI (*fl.* 12TH CENTURY)
42 TRANSLATED BY AZIZ ISA ELKUN
AND RACHEL HARRIS

From *DIWAN-I HIKMET**

Know that Muhammad's essence was Arab,
And on the Path he was the flower of propriety.

He was not a man who did not know the Truth,
Know that there is nothing like him. . . .

His father's name was Abdulla,
And he died before Muhammad was born from his
    mother . . .

When he was seven years old his grandfather died,
And they gave the Prophet to his nurse. . . .

When the Prophet reached the age of forty,
After that revelation came down from God. . . .

[The Prophet said,] 'If you see an orphan do not
    hurt him,
If you see a pauper do not wound him.' . . .

If I describe him, 'Ali is the lion of God,
Who destroys the infidels with his sword. . . .

For Islam 'Ali spilled much blood,
So that the standard of Islam could be firmly held.

He joined Khoja Ahmed and fell into poverty,
The Prophet added his words to those of his
    descendants.

* Despite its name, the *Diwan-i Hikmet* (Collection of Wise
Sayings) is a compilation of poetic narratives organized around
the general theme of Ahmad Yasawi's spiritual biography. The
title probably reflects the fame of Yasawi and his followers as
sheikhs who taught through mystical sayings, but this work
covers more general Islamic knowledge and its description of
Yasawi's life only occasionally embeds his distinctive teachings
within narrated events and dialogues.

LOVE SONG OF NAVA'I (1)

I grieved after I saw your beauty for the first time,
And wished to see your alluring eyes for a second
    time.

Ready to strike with a knife to see you for the third
    time,
I will see on her face a beautiful mole on the fourth
    time we meet.

I will martyr myself for love on the fifth look,
I wish to meet you and see your beautiful eyes for
    a sixth time.

No other beauty like you exists in the seven
    continents,
You are beautiful like a fairy, and I wish to fly over
    you eight times.

When I whirl around you for the ninth time, my body
    will start to burn,
If I try to suppress my soul's will with my ten fingers.

It is eleven months since Nava'i was separated from
    his love,
When it turns twelve months, I will find tranquillity.

ALI-SHIR NAVA'I (1441–1501)
TRANSLATED BY AZIZ ISA ELKUN
AND RACHEL HARRIS

LOVE SONG OF NAVA'I (2)

Fortune's wheel halts heavily before your dark eyes:
My soul suspended in the absence of those eyes.
Life-promising potions concocted into poison
Bringing me nearer to death, unveil your dark eyes.
A world of suitors entranced as you at your loom
    weave
A dream of self. They love you, your ravishing eyes
That once held me close in their wondrous draw,
Now alien beyond my borderland. Your eyes
Burn into mine until brimmed with salt-spiked tears
Which flow, unburdened, into the channels of your eyes.
My very soul solidifies what once was vapor
And vapor becomes friend – your body, your dark eyes.
When Navoiy wrote his poems of yearning love,
Lovers heard him, his songs of dark, infinite eyes.

46 ALI-SHIR NAVA'I (1441–1501)
TRANSLATED BY DENNIS DALY

LOVE SONG OF NAVA'I (3)

Lost in my love's absence, I feel her in my heart:
Her teasing words touch the pulse of my lonely heart.
My eyes redden and blur forever the outside world.
The pain of loss does not recede from a helpless heart.
A nightingale, I swooped from flower to flower;
Now your tresses have snared me, held me to your
    heart.
In the center of this garden, a lovely cypress,
Long-limbed haven, found in flight by trembling
    bird-heart.
Breathless, I search in vain for love's lost tokens,
Remember Farhad and Majnun, death's secrets in
    one heart.
Those who suffer, lovers all, are no different,
Unseen her melody touches those of a same heart.
Navoiy, why do you complain of meetings and
    partings?
Give thanks for those long moments that still fill
    your heart.

LOVE SONG OF NAVA'I (4)

Tulip fields blaze the face of my soul's fire.
Sunsets sear across the sky, touch the earth with fire.
Light radiates through that flesh-façade to essence.
Without fortune and prospect, I ignite with the fire
Of impatience – the guards of prudence have vanished:
My caravan defenseless to the coming fire.
A lightning flash has struck and changed me utterly
As rushes burst and spread in a sea of fire.
Did a whirlwind seize and scatter the flower's life?
Did heaven's treachery envelop in fire
The tapering cypress? How could you do it:
Unveil your countenance, unleash my passion's fire?
Understand, Navoiy, I deny my suffering
As the Masandaran forests turned red with fire.

LOVE SONG OF NAVA'I (5)

God of grief, my love has left, oh my beloved!
She has taken my life, left her distraught beloved –
Propelled through the sky as an arrow leaves the bow,
The long bow of my timid soul. My beloved
Has fled, the strong seeking out the stronger.
Was it my weakness that lost me my beloved?
Take this lesson: avoid the cruelty of love.
I lived love as a beggar to my beloved.
Tell this tale, you who share this suffering with me,
If, in this world of tears, you have found your beloved.
Know this well, Navoiy, your wanderings are to blame:
The same road is now companion to your beloved.

ALI-SHIR NAVA'I (1441–1501)
TRANSLATED BY DENNIS DALY

LOVE SONG OF NAVA'I (6)

Is it the sear of sun that coal-reddens your face,
Or the pleasure of wine that blushes through that
    face?
Is it the glow of innocence that sets like two stars
Those amber drops, accentuating your moon-pearl
    face?
Do you know: perspired beads by the hundreds
Draw me forward like fresh dew drops to your
    petal-face?
Tenderly, you lured me in to thorn impalement,
Blades piercing me, watched by your impassive face.
Was it my heart a-flight that entangled in your locks
That night, or bats blinded to danger: your
    downturned face?
Did dawn dissolve the scent of your dark-haired
    mystery
Or did my sighs flame it from your face?
Afar is beauty an asset to my enemy? –
These thoughts like a poisoned dart, an angered face.
Unaware, perhaps, I've been wounded yet again:
My soul exposed as mortal before your face.
If words could say that Navoiy has turned from your
    love,
Would you believe it? Even those words to your face?

LOVE SONG OF NAVA'I (7)

Save other lovers from heartless empty fate,
Exempt them from this ignominy as I face my fate.
I roam aimless past loose talk and pitying stares,
But let their tongues not blame her for the cruelty
    of fate.
Let no other suffer this unmeasured pain,
Only bearable by me – my personal fate.
Though I have died for my love on numberless days,
Do not mourn my deaths; it will not change your fate.
Build no castles in my heart with your prayers,
Where ruin and fallen parapets predict my fate.
Like the sparkle of a goblet stem, my love blinds me
At night. In the morning there is only a sad fate.
I dream of her and surge with joy she cannot know.
O Navoiy, your desires are nothing: all is fate.

LOVE SONG OF NAVA'I (8)

Her lithe shadow unhugged and lost in night,
Sleep deferred, her promises rule this night.
My eyes follow the onward etch of road;
She has not pierced the depths of distant night.
Perhaps discovery makes her hesitate,
A full moon commands, breathless, over night.
But there were those times without that moon
When darkness filled the starless skies of night.
Strangers may smile at my determined wait
For love; my tears fall into empty night,
Or might have if I had let others see
My naked heart still beating in the night.
Navoiy, Navoiy, pour out a glass of wine,
The sadness of lovers fills up the night.

LOVE SONG OF NAVA'I (9)

Dreaming now of your willowy beauty
Bad luck taunts me. How I love your beauty!
Times over and over I banished you
Forever, but then there was your beauty.
All my desires to possess you mocked,
I offered myself to distant beauty.
You question again my distressed passion,
A present for you – my flawed life – dear beauty.
My troubles mount up in this confused world,
Newfound bothers brought on by your beauty.
Drinking blessed water from Jamshid's goblet
I desire nothing, save your beauty.
Poetry pales before this wretchedness,
Navoiy, we're both prisoners of beauty.

ALI-SHIR NAVA'I (1441–1501)   53
TRANSLATED BY DENNIS DALY

LOVE SONG OF NAVA'I (10)

Petals float down, adorn the path of my dear one.
Has she really returned to join two into one?
I rose from my sick bed to extol her coming,
To laud her approach from afar, my absent one.
The sickness of the lovelorn needs redoubled care,
Also a doctor. Is there a suitable one?
Though hooligans may threaten, may strike at me,
Only she can succeed, she, the pitiless one.
Don't say a miracle-man has come to treat me,
Rather announce my heart's soother: she is the one.
Petitioners have arrived with their dire troubles
But no priceless mention of my beloved one.
Risk not renunciation in the street, Navoiy,
Ask again if she has come, the promised one.

LOVE SONG OF NAVA'I (11)

Loosen your hair, free it, breathe in sweetest heaven
Like a wick loosened ignites a sensuous heaven.
Do you don a flower crown for the sacrifice
Of love? Do you wear the red-spatter from heaven?
Your eyelashes found a fatal spot in my heart,
But instead planted in it the seeds of heaven.
Then did this naked victim fall to love's allure,
A bright shroud thrown over me as I sought heaven.
That day when you unveiled your face and entranced me,
You caught me with beauty between earth and heaven.
Pedagogue of love, you taught me beauty's lessons
Then disregarded my love, destroyed my heaven.
The sultan's closest advisor risks certain doom
If he steals and may forfeit his key to heaven.
Speak up Navoiy, has love injured your very soul?
Do you bleed your love? Is there no help from heaven?

ALI-SHIR NAVA'I (1441–1501)
TRANSLATED BY DENNIS DALY

LOVE SONG OF NAVA'I (12)

Desiring one as fair as a luminous pearl
I dare not utter the elegance of that pearl.
Why wonder if one denies the truth of the world
Or why love bends a man's back before his prized
     pearl.
After too much wine I senselessly rambled on
Craving ruin – an obsession – all for a pearl.
Blown apart in the bilious winds of a tempest
Lightning strikes the outside, inside the priceless
     pearl.
My body in flames fires a path through the night sky,
Yet frets to a reed's width when distant from its pearl.
For many years as a recluse I hid away.
Do dreams and visions come to one seeking life's pearl?
Not surprisingly Navoiy left for the desert
Seeking solace from passion's impregnable pearl.

LOVE SONG OF NAVA'I (13)

Petals adorn nothing without wine's blush of joy.
Why drink wine in the absence of beauty's pure joy?
Miniature suns sparkle out from spotless goblets
But none hears Venus' soft voice imparting its joy.
Do Jupiter, Venus, the sun and moon make sense
If Mars refuses to close that circle of joy?
May the innkeeper of our lives offer us room,
Invite us to the budding realm of latent joy.
Why is the door of happiness locked from inside?
Men must have their wine, savor the moments of joy.
A temperate day to ponder the designs of love
Sits well unless falseness reduces heaven's joy.
Yet even love's absolution for that one day
Denies future pleasures dared and repeated joy.
Treachery roams about, a feral predator.
But in the feast of life we intone to love's joy.
If your fate, Navoiy, lives in your constant prayers
Why would you relinquish your future to blind joy?

ALI-SHIR NAVA'I (1441–1501)
TRANSLATED BY DENNIS DALY

LOVE SONG OF NAVA'I (14)

Arched, so lovely, so resonant with pain,
My heart's deep chasms emitting that pain.
Eyelashes dipped in danger warn me off,
Yet that luminous face belies all pain.
Should I speak of parting or reunion
With her when she delivers me from pain?
Or her cursive words? Or her flowing curls?
Does solicitude or shine curtail pain?
Perhaps it is her changeable spirit
Which allures me, which bestows cutting pain.
Does it do any good to lament fate
Or the world's travails? My heart beats out pain.
Hear me, Navoiy, praise the arches, not the brows,
Laud darkness's depth, not eyes launching pain.

POEMS OF BABUR (1)

The grief of parting from you is like death,
    my dark eyes.
May I come to you with my endless sorrows,
    my dark eyes?
Babur was incapable of soothing his yearning soul,
It is difficult to overcome my suffering, my dark eyes.

I feel contrition when I see the beauty of her hair,
I was astonished when first I glimpsed her face.
Babur must confess he has fallen in love with you,
I am full of regret for anything I have done before.

You are the vital core of my existence, my love,
You are the divine essence of my survival.
Babur has no others as worthy as you, my love,
It's beyond doubt, and you are my life forever.

A man should have to earn his heart's desire,
Or else discard his dreams.
If neither is achieved in this world
He should seek exile in the wilderness.

Shall I tell you about my spirit, full of anguish,
Or the hardships that I have endured during exile?
Have you the courage to stay when my soul sinks into
    sorrow,
Or shall we talk of you, not speaking of my despair?

POEMS OF BABUR (2)

My love, it is not easy to earn your affection,
It is hard to hear tales of your troubles.
I am scarred by my love for you,
And yet I am unable to escape.

I was here before you with a thousand desires, my
    beauty,
For your absence I wrote hundreds of laments.
Why are you not my soulmate on the journey of life?
I could ease your misery, and unite with your bitter
    love.

Though you have given me fortitude through love
You have also condemned me to the pain of separation.
I implore you, make me as powerful as Nava'i
As though you were contacting a man already dead.

The world stands before you as an enemy and makes
    you suffer,
And the wine of arrogance will make you drunk for
    days.
But fear not, it allows you to reach the heavens
And ultimately, brings you back down to earth.

Desire torments my heart; what shall I do?
My heart trembles because of our separation; tell me,
    what shall I do?
My body is tortured with agonizing spasms; what shall
    I do?
My life is full of terrible wickedness; tell me, what shall
    I do?

POEMS OF BABUR (3)

In my perpetual absence, be at peace
And free your wounded soul from suffering.
I have written this to you with the sole purpose
That you recall me when you discern me in these
    lines.

I will remember you always for your letter
I left my eyes behind as I fell in love with you.
I will fashion a quill from your eyelashes
Then from your irises I will make the ink.

It is my desire to see your beauty every day
The scent of your hair is always in my dreams.
The breath of Jesus will give me strength and
    inspiration
I hope the spring wind can bring news of your grief.

This shattered soul is healing while earning your love
My life is inspired after seeing your beautiful face.
Despite the trauma of expulsion clouding my vision
I am joyful when hearing your words and seeing you
    in my dreams.

I have been waiting years for this outcome
And have devoted immense effort to achieving it.
You need courage for good fortune to come
I will surrender you to God, then entrust you this
    country.

POEMS OF BABUR (4)

My love, you have neglected my sorrowful soul
You have rejected my passion and offered me no
    indulgence.
Have you forgotten me because of my mistakes?
Do you no longer feel my absence after our quarrels?

I hope to hear about my lover on the dawn wind
Come to me as a breeze and whirl around my head.
If you ask me not to come to you as before
Then I will approach and lay my head at your feet.

Why do we suffer the pain of separation?
We will enjoy the fruition of our desires.
God will bless you when you come to me
Show your soul's mercy to my devotion.

Remember our love story, let us start afresh
Let us live with the ache of love and rejoice in
    ourselves.
You said I should not forget you during my exile
How could I ever forget you and yet recall the rest?

It should not be surprising if flowers and thorns exist
    together
It should not be surprising if drops of blood are made
    of pearls.
If some foolishness in my poems irks you, I beg
    forgiveness
But do not be surprised at either good or bad verse.

POEMS OF BABUR (5)

Do not tear me down, my beautiful love
Do not condemn me to endless separation.
Blessed God, I have trusted in your goodness
Be merciful, O moon! Do not leave me hopeless.

In this exile, I cannot endure the bloodshed
    in my wake
It is impossible to stop my tears, even for a moment.
The sun is witness to my suffering
And in God's name, I will not forget anything.

One who does good deeds, receives kindness in return
One who oppresses, receives that self-same
    tribulation.
No good person deserves misery or torment
An evil person merits chastisement and disgrace.

I have suffered agonies because of my cursed fate
I have done all I can, but it has ended in
    transgression.
I am facing the dilemma of India, and must abandon
    that tired place
Despite all of this, great God, please do not take away
    my good fate.

For a long time, I have lived without my soulmate
I breathe, but I have no one to console me.
I have arrived at sadness of my own free will
Babur, there is little left of your ill fate.

ZAHIR-UD-DIN MUHAMMAD BABUR (1483–1530)   63
TRANSLATED BY AZIZ ISA ELKUN

POEMS OF BABUR (6)

I have heard that Jamshid, the magnificent,
Inscribed on a rock at a fountain-head
'Many men like us have taken breath at this fountain,
And have passed away in the twinkling of an eye.
We took the world by courage and might,
But we took it not with us to the tomb.'

ZAHIR-UD-DIN MUHAMMAD BABUR (1483–1530)
64   TRANSLATED BY ANNETTE SUSANNAH
BEVERIDGE

LOVE GHAZAL OF MASHRAB (1)

I suffer from dusk until dawn, pleading at your
    doorstep
I long to give my life away to you, princess, to leave
    it at your doorstep.

Your scent is of ravishing blooms like jasmine or
    white roses
And a glorious green pine tree grows at your
    doorstep.

Your beauty has enraptured me, and my life is at risk
A hunter seeks his beloved bird of life and prays at
    your doorstep.

While I sought you, I was consumed with the lunacy
    of love
When I saw your fierce eyes, this pain felled me at
    your doorstep.

I shed tears night and day because of this cruel
    separation
The country is being destroyed, regardless of the
    blossom at your doorstep.

The fire of your beauty had already caught and burnt
    Mashrab
I was like a moth drawn to a flame, my beloved, at
    your doorstep.

LOVE GHAZAL OF MASHRAB (2)

Love has stricken me, turned me raving
The people scorn and mock me, despairing.

Oh, when searching for love, I cry with blood
From my tears, all the continents start to flood.

You must avoid leaving your love in sadness
You have caused me misery, you are heartless.

I yearn for you every day, even when you bring great
    pain
Observe the stone of my agony, I withstand this force
    like a chain.

Mashrab has made the entire palace surprised
Why did you not come to have a look inside?

LOVE GHAZAL OF MASHRAB (3)

Every wretched man should be brave enough to cry
    before his love
He should confess all to her, leaving nothing in his
    heart to atone for.

Like a nightingale which has lost its voice, suffering
    and gasping
He shuns the garden where he once sang and keeps
    wandering.

If every man faced the challenge of avoiding drinking
On judgment day, he could give his account before the
    Jabbar.*

Mashrab, you are an apprentice; never reveal your
    secrets to religious men
If you do, you shall return to your love writhing,
    moaning and crying.

* One of the names of God in Islam.

LOVE GHAZAL OF MASHRAB (4)

I want to tell my sorrows to the winds of dawn
Give our blessings to the beloved soulmate.

Through morning-star eyes, your alluring figure
    vanishes
You have filled me with anguish and pain, my black
    eyes.

Her beauty was astounding, but she was deceitful
She never kept the promises she made to me.

She flew away from me before my very eyes
She departed, hurling me into eternal grief.

We came to an agreement to place this misery
Before our God, to decide which of us was at fault.

The pain of loving you has left me ailing
Where do I go to complain about my torment?

I did everything for you to earn your love
Has God witnessed my enduring suffering?

I will beg for her, oh my beloved
I will not be tortured with this heartache.

LOVE GHAZAL OF MASHRAB (5)

The pain I endured gave me the wings and tail of
    a bird
And my haunted, loving soul soared up into the sky.

My enemies have denied me victory
I set off on the road facing hazards and adversity.

My love, you are merciless and deceitful
You were never kind to this broken man.

Endless pain has turned my face sallow
My complexion adds a hue to the garden of Eden.

My heartless love, I am aflame for you
I submit all my grievances to almighty God.

My beloved, if I could see your beauty
I would dedicate my life to your adoration.

I am burning with great passion, my beautiful love
Please be merciful this once; I have become lovelorn.

Why would Mashrab not lament when he suffers?
The eyes of the executioners are on me.

LOVE GHAZAL OF MASHRAB (6)

In the desert of despair I cried, where is my beloved one?
Wracked with anguish I asked, where is the nightingale
of my garden?

I may or may not be a betrayer, but I will never plead
for your mercy
Whatever befalls, stay strong, oblivious to accusations
of evil.

I wandered far and wide and found you, my flower
garden
After great amazement, I returned to my house of
despair.

Our parting left scars upon my soul, my ruthless love,
Tears are falling from my eyes like a hail of blood.

I have no lover. To whom am I meant to lament my
sorrow?
Is there anybody kind enough to hear me with
compassion?

I exist in an awful state, nobody knows of me
My travails have pierced the roof of the sky.

Why can I not force my miserable heart to feel any joy?
My beloved was here, but she did not feel my heartache.

Oh my true love, be tender and ask about me
Why, when I look your way, do my eyes become
fountains?

70   BABA RAHIM MASHRAB (1657–1711)
TRANSLATED BY AZIZ ISA ELKUN

LOVE GHAZAL OF MASHRAB (7)

Like a grieving nightingale I alighted in the flower
    garden
As I came there, the sorrow in my soul turned into
    fragrance.

My distressed soul will never bloom like the petals of
    a flower
Hoping the pain in my heart would vanish, I came to
    Khotan.*

My pupils were dejected at the thought of separation,
My desires unfulfilled, I came back to my home.

The people here believe that Mashrab's every
    utterance is priceless
I am known for my beautiful words; so here I came.

* Khotan (Hotan) is a major historical oasis city in the south-
west of the Uyghur homeland.

LOVE GHAZAL OF MASHRAB (8)

Burning with love for Sanam, the weary Mashrab has
wandered and suffered
Wretched tearful eyes, and a soul shattered into
numberless pieces: Mashrab.

Careless, I pay not the slightest attention to this
merciless world
For the sake of love, I am ready to abandon these two
worlds, the resentful Mashrab.

Even when I meet death, the pain of your love will not
leave my tomb
I can find no remedy for my grief; I have become the
broken Mashrab.

Since my mother gave birth to me, I have suffered for
your love
I have been trekking through the desert of love,
grieving, the troubled Mashrab.

I was gifted a wine goblet of love; I had no other
option but to drink
My tears ran red, not ceasing, my veins filled with
blood, the destitute Mashrab.

While I endure a thousand dangers, I beg for
blessings from the Saint
If you cut out my tongue, fear not, 'We will meet
again,' said the enduring Mashrab.

Wherever I go, people are shocked, and chase me
    from town to town
I have missed countless opportunities yet stand with
    courage, the mad, bothersome Mashrab.

I am nameless to people wherever I go, no one knows
    who I truly am
I devote myself to the passions of my heart, how
    subtle and clever, the wanderer Mashrab.

I beg for your kindness to this solitary nomad, the
    roaming Mashrab
Who has abandoned prayer and fasting during
    Ramadan, the stumbling Mashrab.

LOVE GHAZAL OF MASHRAB (9)

Show your beauty to the one who adores you,
To the moth that burns for your love.

If you consent to my prayer,
My life will be dedicated to love.

Oh, you are cruel, you show no mercy,
Cast a glance upon this unfortunate one.

I am a love-stricken man; show your affection at last,
To this madman who is burning for your love.

Mashrab has given up his life for you,
And placed his head on your doorstep.

BABA RAHIM MASHRAB (1657–1711)
74 TRANSLATED BY AZIZ ISA ELKUN
AND RACHEL HARRIS

LOVE GHAZAL OF MASHRAB (10)

If I left the city of Namangan, would anyone visit me?
If I went wandering in the city of loneliness, would
     anyone visit me?

Where are my brothers, will they serve as companions
     on my way?
If I was weeping, would anyone visit me?

I drank a cordial of love, and boiled over like a pot,
If I renounce this world, will anyone visit me?

Madness has come over me, and love's fire is burning,
If I devote myself to this, will anyone visit me?

I have no patience left to stay, and I cannot leave,
With this fierce fire burning in my heart, will anyone
     visit me?

I can't decide if I should stay in Namangan, or go
     wandering,
If I go wandering around the world, will anyone
     visit me?

No one knows how much poor Mashrab has suffered,
If I leave this place, will anyone visit me?

BABA RAHIM MASHRAB (1657–1711)
TRANSLATED BY AZIZ ISA ELKUN
AND RACHEL HARRIS

A GHAZAL OF ZELILI

They say you are the most beautiful of all flowers,
They say you are a beggar burning with the madness
of love.

Don't be surprised, oh princess, that I stay day and
night at your door,
Whenever I create a melody for you, they say, you are
tuneless.

Do not feel amused when you look at the graveyard,
After they place you in your grave, they say, all will
mourn for you.

You have left a stain on the young soul of a flowery
land,
You amuse yourself, but those who have seen the
wilderness say that you are misfortune.

I went to the healer and asked where I could find a
cure for my heartache,
But the healer said, you foolish man, there is no cure
for your illness.

Zelili smeared on his face the dust from under the
hooves of your horse,
The echo of a voice comes from your palace, it says,
rub it into your eyes.

A GHAZAL OF GUMNAM

When I saw your eyebrows, how could I not feel
     thrilled, for you set the direction of my prayers,
How could I not place my head beneath your feet, for
     you are my place of worship?
How could I not surrender my soul and give up this
     beautiful life in order to kiss your lips,
How could I not open wide my eyes when I saw your
     face, beautiful like a full moon?

The flames of sorrow struck me and raged in my head
Though I am a poor man, I wear a golden crown.

When you hide your face, it is as though a cloud has
     blocked the sun
It's not your hair but your face that makes me fear the
     pain of fire.

In the garden, not among the stars, a flower lies
     drenched in blood
My heart roams across the earth and sky searching
     for your beauty.

I do not fear my enemies; I overcome them in the
     blink of an eye
If your eyebrows were my enemies, they would
     destroy me.

I have lost my soul, that is certain, but I am uncertain
     about you
When I found the jewel of love, I surrendered to its
     sweetness.

MUHAMMAD EMIN GHOJAMQULI GUMNAM   77
(1633–1724), TRANSLATED BY AZIZ ISA ELKUN

A GHAZAL OF NAZIMI

Fate has separated us; where are you dear brother?
Since I have been parted from you, the food I eat is
   poison.

My heart is broken and my soul is wounded, I am so
   pitiful,
Good fortune has gone and misery has come,
   suffering is my companion.

My kind brother has gone, my roots have abandoned
   me,
Because of this separation, my tears flow like the
   blood in my veins.

I wander the streets weeping, making trouble for
   myself,
I don't know what I am doing, my mind whirls with
   grief.

How can I be patient after losing you? Sadness grips
   my heart,
Suffering such grief, my soul explodes with bitterness.

MOLLA BILAL NAZIMI (1824–1900)
TRANSLATED BY AZIZ ISA ELKUN
AND RACHEL HARRIS

From *GHERIP AND SANAM* *
Uyghur folk epic

[Princess Sanam laments the absence of her lover]

'The bird of fortune flew away from me,
No trace of its whereabouts.
I searched for it from winter to summer,
But there was no sign of it anywhere.

'I let my heroic bird fly.
Few knew about my lover
And no one knows where he has flown to.
I will not stop until I find him.

'I wish that my lover
Would come and take away my misery.
If our cruel enemy discovers us,
There will be no place for us to hide.

'The world will be a place of war for us,
Whom will we tell of our heartache?
We hope it will turn like an autumn leaf and fall.
There is no destination on the road of love.

'If I could but stay an hour on the road of love,
If I could but hold my lover's hand . . .
But I must cross the desert for my love,
And my heart has no strength left.'

Princess Sanam said, 'Oh, my darling,
Don't bring trouble on yourself.
I beg you, end this suffering soon,
Our souls have no strength left.

'Dear brothers and friends,
Why doesn't my lover come?
My life is burning in love's fire,
Why doesn't my lover come?

' "I will come", he promised,
Now he has left me grieving.
Soon it will be noon,
Why doesn't my lover come?

'I long to see his beautiful face,
To walk with him side by side.
Our time together is always joyful,
Why doesn't my lover come?

'Suffering upon suffering,
My soul is filled with sorrow and misery.
The flower in my hand has wilted,
Why doesn't my lover come?

'The food I eat is poison,
My clothes are a winding sheet,
My face has become pale.
Why doesn't my lover come?

'He may have suffered some misfortune,
He may have been captured
Or locked in prison.
Why doesn't my lover come?

'My heart has been torn apart,
Is there a way to end this pain?
Helpless Gherip is weeping,
Why doesn't my lover come?'

Gherip and Sanam is an epic love tale of separation, suffering
and eventual reunion, which has transmitted orally among
the Uyghurs since the sixteenth century, and also, in different
versions, among other Turkic peoples, including Uzbeks,
Azerbaijanis and Turkmens. The earliest handwritten copy
was made by Haji Yusuf in 1873–4 in Kashgar, and many
modern versions have since been published. The tale is also
found in the lyrics of the Uyghur Twelve Muqam. A modern
opera based on *Gherip and Sanam* was created by Qasimjan
Qemberi in the early twentieth century and it was produced as
a film in 1982 by the Xinjiang and Shanghai Film Studios.

THE SONG OF YAQUB BEG*
Uyghur folk lyrics

Is there any man like Yaqub Beg?
Was any city built like his?
When Yaqub Beg sets out on a campaign,
Will any enemy be left alive?

Listen, great fighters,
Get ready for battle.
The enemy has arrived,
Get ready for battle.

Yaqub Beg is a hero,
When he attacked the enemy
The heads of Chinese soldiers
Lay like pebbles on the ground.

Yaqub Beg went hunting,
He rode a fast horse.
After Yaqub Beg died
There was turmoil for five days.

The gates of the new city
Were sometimes open, sometimes closed.
Lord Yaqub Beg –
Where will we find another like him?

The angels in the sky
Wore fairy robes.
Ladies, do not shed your tears,
Yaqub Beg lives in heaven.

The gourds of Aqsu
Flourish in the shade.
The dear people of Kashgar
Flourished under Yaqub Beg.

The Chinese arrived from Beijing,
Showing their fake smiles.
Our lords and officials ran away,
Showing their tails behind.

The people of Kashgar were martyred.
Yaqub Beg was our ruler;
After we parted from Yaqub Beg
Our people began to suffer.

Yaqub Beg stood for justice,
He treated the people fairly.
Now where can we find
A man like our lord Yaqub Beg?

* Yaqub Beg was born in Pishkent in 1820. After several
years of war against the Manchu Qing Empire, Yaqub Beg
expelled their soldiers, eliminated Manchu control over the
Uyghur region, and established himself as ruler of the State
of Kashgaria. He fostered close diplomatic relationships with
the British and Ottoman Empires and played a significant
role during the Great Game between the British, Russian and
Manchu Qing Empires. According to Sayrami, a historian
of the time, he was poisoned and died on 30 May 1877. In
1884 the whole region was reoccupied by the Chinese, and
the Uyghur homeland was officially renamed 'Xinjiang'
(New Frontier). These anonymous folk lyrics were collected
from Uyghurs in Kazakhstan in the mid-twentieth century.

TRANSLATED BY AZIZ ISA ELKUN

THE MIGRATION *
Extracts from Ili folk-song lyrics

When we decided to leave
We made boats.
The White Khan and the Black Khan†
Were in alliance all along.

You will go to an oasis, they said,
But we went to a place like a desert.
They did not speak the truth,
The blue-eyed, hairy-headed ones.

Russian carts
Have small wheels at the front.
Living in another's land
It is hard to pass the days.

The soldiers of the White Khan
Cut stone and dig for gold.
They force farmers to migrate, threatening
To cut off their heads with a sword.

Are they afraid of migrating,
People who have never left home?
Will it be a better place than their own,
A place they have never seen?

When I sat at the food stall
They brought my food on a plate.
When I thought of Ili
Tears welled up in my black eyes.

The people who set out on the journey
Headed towards the west.
They bade farewell to their homeland,
Tears in their eyes.

Brothers, at last, farewell,
God keep you safe.
If we live
We will meet again one day in peace.

As we left on our carts
We took one more look behind us.
We were the unlucky ones,
Separated from our parents.

My black horse was once a foal,
Now it has grown and become a horse.
My cousins whom we left behind at home
Have become strangers to us.

When we started our migration from Ili
It was June, and the month of Ramadan.
During those hard days
We wished we had our parents with us.

They say that on the road to Yarkent
There are rocks blocking the bridge.
He who forced us to leave home,
Tsar Nikolas, has no mercy.

There is a wasteland near Yarkent,
You should visit that place.
You have brought upon us these hardships,
You will suffer one day yourself.

* *Köch-köch* (The Migration) is a body of orally transmitted
folk literature that depicts the historical forced migrations
of the Uyghur people under the Manchu Qing Empire and
under the Russian Empire. In the seventeenth and eighteenth
centuries, large numbers of Uyghur families were moved from
the southern regions of Aqsu, Yarkand and Kashgar into the
northern Ili Valley by the Manchu Qing administration. In
the 1860s the Russians briefly controlled the Ili Valley, and
following their departure in the 1880s around 10,000 Uyghurs
moved across the border into what is now Kazakhstan. Some of
the families who moved to Russia later fled back to the Uyghur
homeland in the 1930s during Stalin's Terror. This particular
set of lyrics was collected among Uyghurs in Kazakhstan
in the mid-twentieth century, and refers to the nineteenth-
century migration into present-day Kazakhstan.

† White Khan = Russian Tsar; Black Khan = Chinese Emperor

UYGHUR FOLK POEMS
From the collection by Gunnar Jarring[*]

Among these roses
I saw your sign
I have to let you know
I've fallen in love with you.

I gave you an apple, but you refused to take it
I gave you a quince, but you didn't take it
What kind of rich man's daughter are you
You don't even glance at me?

The fierce tiger lies on the road
It won't give way to the lion
Those who are cursed by their parents
Will never thrive.

That swallow is so black
May it never lose its wings
That girl is so delicate
She should never leave her mother.

I will serve the food myself
My black eyes are crying
If my darling is unhappy with me
I am ready to apologize.

My flower is gone, she is gone
My nightingale flew away from my hand
In this short life
Who can achieve their goal?

My darling didn't go to the wedding
How could I go without asking her
My darling's heart is so sensitive
Even serving her tea won't make her smile.

Come, my darling, let's play
Let's walk along the riverbank
Let's complain to the fish
Let's cry to God.

I'll count the flowers
On your embroidered hat
When will you come, my darling
I'm watching the road for you.

When clouds cover the sky
The moon will be hidden
There's doubt in my heart
I won't get to kiss my darling.

I am yours, only yours
Who would I belong to except you?
I am the slave
That you bought in Kashgar.

* These Uyghur folk verses were collected by the Swedish
Turkologist Gunnar Jarring (1907–2002) between 1929
and 1930 when he came to Eastern Turkistan to conduct
research on Uyghur folklore. Jarring was a board member of
the Swedish Oriental Society 1936–40 and lectured at Lund
University 1939–41.

MODERN POEMS

THE NIGHT OF TURPAN

Why is it so humid and hot?
Why is the night of Turpan so airless?
As though trapped in a cage I cannot draw breath
The night of Turpan will make you sweat.

When the valley brings in the hot wind
Babies cry in their cradles
Mothers softly croon their lullabies
Why is the night of Turpan so airless?

Stars twinkle in the sky
Flowers wilt in the garden
People fan themselves and complain
Why is the night of Turpan so airless?

Mulberry trees seem to shed tears
Like the young and old weeping in the city
When is the new day going to begin?
The night of Turpan is lightless.

When the day breaks, golden light shines
Don't doubt whether the sun will rise
There is a beam of light shining from the horizon
But still the night of Turpan goes by, seamless.

Turpan, 1922

ABDUHALIQ UYGHUR (1901–33)   91
TRANSLATED BY AZIZ ISA ELKUN

TO BLOOM

My flowers are ready to bloom
Soon I can wear them as a crown
The fire of my love
Is going to engulf my entire soul.

My love flirts with me
She laughs and she mocks me
You don't know how precious this love is
She can turn the cold winter to summer.

We suffer for our love
Through love, we are ground down like flour
Through terror, we become hard as stone
Without unity, we scatter like sand.

Oh, our young generation, do not fall asleep
Don't be an obstacle to our love
I am ready to sacrifice myself for my love
Grateful for every step you have taken.

My courageous flower, let's bloom
All the efforts I made, let them bloom
If I am giving up my life for my beloved
It is because we will one day die anyway.

To live or die
My love, let's bloom.

A CALL BEFORE DEATH

We must always be ready to face life or death
The fear of death makes us worthless
Ready to lift our heads
and stand with a courageous gesture.

If I die in battle, I hope one day my flowers will
    bloom!

Turpan, 13 March 1933

ABDUHALIQ UYGHUR (1901–33)
TRANSLATED BY AZIZ ISA ELKUN

ANSWER TO THE YEARS

Time is hastening by, it will not tarry for you
The year is one of time's swiftest sprinters
Running water and bygone dawns will never return
The running years are the greatest thief of life.

They steal away and run without a backward glance
They pursue each other, in a frantic race
When nightingales cease to flap their wings in
    youth's garden
The leaves will wilt and then begin to fall.

Youth is humanity's best season
Although its time on earth is very brief
When a page is torn from the calendar
A petal falls from the flower of youth.

When the wind of time blows, tracks will be covered
And the poor bare trees, without leaves, will shrivel
But the years are not empty-handed, for they bring
Laugh lines for the girls and beards for the boys.

But please do not be angry with the years
Accept that they will pass along their way
Those who do not let time slip through their fingers
Theirs are the hands that make an oasis from a desert.

The years' embrace is vast, and the opportunities are
        many
Jobs the size of mountains will be completed in these
        years
Behold the baby who arrived two nights ago
He started crawling yesterday and today he's walking.

The children of the revolution are chasing the years
The revolution will surely find their grandchildren
Those who sacrificed themselves last night for a
        better life
Will surely have their gravestones bedecked with
        flowers.

Let the years bless me with a beard
During these years I will refine myself
I will place the stamp of my poems
On the neck of each year that runs before me.

I will not get old at the peak of revolution
My poems will shine like stars before me
Loitering in the midst of revolution is like death
I want to be victorious with patience and courage.

I will hold those hands, which are trained to shoot
        rifles
I will march along the road with my flag aloft
I will never tire of the revolutionary battle
Only in victory will we reach the wide road.

Hey years! Don't split your sides laughing
I'd sooner die than stand ashamed before you
Don't think about making me any older
I will prepare my son for the final war.

Though the sea of years is immeasurably vast
Our warship will cross your horizon
Though the passing years may threaten us
We will answer them with our deeds and
    make them old.

Aqsu, January 1944

TRANSLATED BY AZIZ ISA ELKUN

A THOUGHTFUL WISH

I am not frustrated, and I wish you all the best,
    my friends
But the sleeves that I rolled up for the revolution
    I will never pull down.

A clever orchard keeper never allows his orchard to
    be parched
Or lets his trees perish for want of caring.

My wish is like the innocent dream of a child
Who constantly desires its mother's breast.

Staring at the sky full of sweet appreciation
I can see the horizon clearly with sharp, thoughtful
    eyes.

My love is sleeping sweetly, but why is she not
    moving?
While I wait outside, opening the small windows
    for light

I am ever thoughtful . . . I became melancholy as
    a youth
From listening to my grandmother's mystical tales.

Because I am a wave of love drawn deep from the sea
How can I slake my thirst, drinking water from
    puddles?

Aqsu, June 1945

LUTPULLA MUTELLIP (1922–45)   97
TRANSLATED BY AZIZ ISA ELKUN

THE LAST WORD*

This world has become a living hell for me,
This bloodthirsty devil has turned the bloom of my
    youth into a withered leaf . . .

Aqsu, September 1945

* This poem was written by the poet on the wall with his
blood before he was executed by the Chinese police in Aqsu in
September 1945. He was only twenty-two years old.

TO MY DAUGHTER, THE WAR NURSE*

You steeled yourself to break from slavery,
You did not flee from bombs, guns, or cannon.
You cleansed our revered country of brutal foes,
My precious daughter – war nurse.

Standing armed on the front line like a brave man,
You advanced into battle with such ferocity.
You hovered like a planet in the sky,
Your life became an offering, my hero, war nurse.

Liberty and independence blazed in your heart,
You bestowed your young life on people and country.
You gave hope to soldiers in the heat of battle,
A sacrifice for the valiant, my daughter, war nurse.

Oh Rizwangul, your voice was like a ringing bell,
Your beauty was that of a rosebud.
Your glorious name is forever in our history,
You are alive – lover of freedom, my daughter, war nurse.

January 1945

* This poem was dedicated to a young Uyghur war nurse called
Rizwangul, who died on 13 January 1945 during an attempt by
the East Turkistan National Army to liberate the city of Ghulja
from the Chinese Nationalist Army. She was nineteen years
old when she was killed on the front line rescuing wounded
soldiers, and she has become a symbol of the struggle to free
East Turkistan from Chinese occupation. Qasimjan Qemberi
published this poem in the 'Liberated East Turkistan' newspaper
on 20 January 1945. The East Turkistan Republic held power
until October 1949, when it was forced by Stalin to join the newly
established People's Republic of China.

QASIMJAN QEMBERI (1910–56)   99
TRANSLATED BY MUNAWWAR ABDULLA

YOUR OPPORTUNITY

Opportunity awaits, we plunge headlong onto broiling
    battle,
We will rescue our people from the tyrants'
    massacres.
Ili has awoken; the nights of terror spread . . .
We will liberate the nation they seek to destroy.

My love, though you have vanished from my soul,
May this land be a shelter for the men who march to
    battle.
We flew high like falcons, now, wielding powerful
    weapons,
With your favour we will win through and cross the
    Tengritagh.*

May the hearts of lovers never be disturbed,
Like Eden's nightingales, may we carol for joy.
Oh Lord, Tengri! from the heavens, hear my cry,
Grant us triumph, let us free our motherland soon.

We have defeated, and will defeat again the evil,
  vicious foe,
We will make unhappy souls rejoice.
We aim to plant our flag in Shingshiysa,[†]
The opportunity is here, soon we will reach our goal!

May 1945

* Tengritagh – the Heavenly Mountains – is a mountain
range spanning the centre of East Turkistan. It is also part
of Central Asia's most prominent and extended system of
mountain ranges. Tengri was the supreme deity in the religion
of Tengrism which was prevalent in the region before the
coming of Islam; 'tengri' can also refer to the sky. 'Tagh'
means mountain.

† Shingshiysa is a Chinese border town between China and
East Turkistan.

FOR THE HOMELAND

Sharing the suffering of your homeland
Is the equivalent of a monarch's throne.

If you can reduce your people's suffering by one
    moment
It will be equal to a millennium of prosperity.

The world goes by like this
Before you perish, you should leave behind a legacy.

What is a valuable legacy? It's serving your people
A good reputation is not about making a fortune.

If your people require you to sacrifice your life
It would be best if you do so graciously.

If you work hard and walk onward with success
Then you will be able to leave a mark on history.

In this era, the age of dishonour
You have to live as a courageous man.

Life is full of hardship and struggle
You have to be able to overcome obstacles.

Successful people will make many enemies
You will have to bury them in the dust.

Rather than live false-heartedly like a fox
Be honourable and die as a lion.

Written in 1947

102   AHMED ZIYA'I (1913–89)
    TRANSLATED BY AZIZ ISA ELKUN

BEFORE

I need nothing aside from the love of my beloved
You are the greatest hope of my soul and body
In a land of gardens you are the finest rose
I would visit you if I only had the chance
Let my face be shamed before the glory of the dawn.

Nothing in this world compares to the stones of your
    mountains
For you on those stones I would pile up your enemies'
    heads
For you I would make their tears flow like rivers
If I could only see your moon-like eyebrows
Then my dark fate would be gleaming before gracious
    God.

One tragic day came the tread of those wicked
    enemies
Who rain down blows on beautiful fairies like you
In your embrace I felt such a sense of agony
I was deprived of your abundant pleasures
Like a cat tied up in a granary in front of a mouse.

I will return, my love, never lose hope
Keep striking at your enemies, never let them go free
Don't be fooled, don't join the feast with your
    adversary
Don't let the enemy pick fruit from my orchard
Soon we will find each other in the land of flowers.

I will not be a man until I shed your enemy's blood
Until I pin the traitors' guilt upon their chests
Until I see them stung with their own poison
Until I lull them all to sleep in the cradle of the
  ground
Only then will I earn a hero's name to rival
  Shahimerdan's.*

Though our enemies kill without mercy before
  I return
Though their bloodthirsty swords gleam above
  my lover's head
Though in their cruelty they lose all humanity
I will take revenge while my heart beats in my body
For a man can never be defeated by a vicious beast.

Ghulja, November 1947

* Shahimerdan is a legendary hero of Central Asian people.

I WILL REMEMBER YOU

The nightingales sing amongst the flowers,
I will remember you with a powerful song.
My darling, I am your besotted flower,
I will miss you every day at dawn.

When the breeze plays with my flowing hair,
I ask whether my love has arrived.
Because the cords of my heart are linked to you
With desire, I seek you every day at dawn.

The clouds take joy in chasing the stars,
The stars laugh, twinkling their eyes.
I will always remember your proud gestures
When I am pining for you, my dear love.

MELIKE ZIYAWUDUN (1938–70)
TRANSLATED BY AZIZ ISA ELKUN

TOP SECRET

I always read your poems,
I can see you are my soulmate from your poems,
How sweet your every verse,
I learned your secrets from your poems.

Each word in your poems burns like a flame,
They enter my heart and start to burn.
With passion I commit them to my memory,
They become the pearls in the soul of my sea.

I always love your poems, my darling,
Not just your poems but perhaps you as well.
If you are clever, you'll know this is top secret,
Look into my eyes, and you'll know, my dear.

September 1957

AWAITING SPRING

In the candle flame the moth burns itself bravely,
For your fair face, my love, I would sacrifice myself.

Once you came smiling, the flower garden was filled
    with your love,
Where have those days gone, now I have become a
    wanderer?

For your love I become a madman, burning out like
    a candle nightly,
My body melts, and tears pour from my eyes like
    pearls.

My hair grows long, a stick in my hand, my dim eyes
    gaze down the road,
If anyone met me now, they would be dismayed.

I yearn to see your beautiful face once, without
    placing my head at your feet,
Will I always endure this suffering, will this life pass
    in sorrow?

If my home were illuminated by your radiant beauty
That good fortune would remain with me forever.

A speck of dirt cannot fall onto the surface of the sun;
    the wing of hope will never break,
If I lose my desire for you, I will become a beggar
    wandering the world.

Following Nava'i's trail of misery, I see my beloved's
    reflection in the wine,
Holding a wine cup in my hand, I go from one wine
    shop to the next.

Urumchi, 30 March 1970

TRANSLATED BY AZIZ ISA ELKUN

I AM NOT A WHITE FLAG

Khan Tengri* is a heavenly mountain
With a peak that reaches through the sky, shines
Like silver and pearls, so proud
The sun rises from the East, kisses the mountain,
Cheek against cheek, passes along
And travels West, away from the peak
On a full moon, the Seven Stars, Mercury,
Saturn, and Jupiter descend for a visit,
And before parting, bow to the mountain
White riverbeds of ice, the snow never melts,
Summer, winter, nature beats in his chest, breaks
Through the stones: a miracle snow orchid grows
The peak is a beautiful white flower,
On a spring day, a swan on a lake
The man from afar doesn't know
Such strength, says it is the flag of surrender
Khan Tengri hears this, laughs loudly and says,
'Where are you from? Listen, ignorant man,
Beyond question, I am not a white flag
My beard may be white, my hair, my face,
White, though make no mistake, I
Am not a white flag
I am the firstborn child of Adam and Eve
I am both Heaven and Earth
When Noah floundered in the flood without hope,
I was the dove he released, returning with the
        olive twig

When double-horned Alexander brought violence
To the land, it was I who blocked his path
Trade caravans on the Silk Road, bells chiming
      faintly,
There I was beside them, their guardian along history
For I completed the words in the Book of History,
Unknotting the many, so many, mysteries of the past
Paper, compass, printing, and the wonder
Of gunpowder, passing through me, expanding
The world's moment
I rocked the cradle of civilization since time began
I have been here, from all-knowing Earth's prime
Moment and so my head is as white as my coat,
      but a white
Flag I will never become, no matter what you do
O great motherland, on which my life depends wholly,
The whiteness of hair and beard, the foundation of
      history
Peak reaching through the sky, the sign of the
      mother-
Land, if clouds obstruct or lightning strikes, still
I stand firmly
My head doesn't bend; I do not sway
How, then, did I become a white flag to you?
My heart is red fire, and I lift a blue flag with dignity;
I march boldly in ancientness, singing
My song of victory that echoes the world

You, have you forgotten the centuries,
The years of my sustenance, collecting
My treasures, that you in shameless ingratitude
See me as a white flag?'

* Tengritagh, also known as Khan Tengri, holds a significant
place in the hearts of the Uyghur people and is a majestic
symbol in the heart of their homeland. This awe-inspiring
mountain range divides the vast landscape into the North
and South, serving as a cultural and political emblem for the
Uyghur nation. With a remarkable span of 2,500 kilometres,
it claims the title of both the longest and highest mountain
range in the region. Its journey begins in the Qomul region in
the eastern part of the Uyghur homeland, and ends far away in
the south-western regions of Kyrgyzstan and Kazakhstan. The
grandeur of Tengritagh is not confined to its physical stature;
it embodies the spirit and resilience of the Uyghur people,
representing their enduring connection to the land and their
rich cultural heritage.

ABDUREHIM ÖTKÜR (1923–95)
TRANSLATED BY DOLKUN KAMBERI
AND JEFFREY YANG

I CALL FORTH SPRING

Weary souls, out of the dead of winter,
From the depths of my soul, I call forth spring.
In the late evening, like a roaring lion,
With my bitter cries, I call forth spring.

No longer have I patience nor restraint,
My heart is now a boiling pot.
As if my hope were now a volcano,
And from that volcano, I call forth spring.

This ceaseless weeping here in fear of death,
This flood of tears – were these our legacy?
To keep one's head bowed is a traitor's work,
With my clear conscience, I call forth spring.

These praises I sing, even in dead of winter,
Even though my tongue be bound in chains,
Though spears be fixed upon my breast,
With my warm blood, I call forth spring.

I call forth spring, I call forth spring,
I wish for a lover to bring the people joy.
My dream is spring, my hope is spring,
And with no other will I share my heart.

I call forth spring, I call forth spring,
This is the people's sorrow – this I praise.
It was my grandfather who taught me this,
Why ever should I love anything else?

I call forth spring in the late evening,
Even if my budding life should wither.
To this I agree: there is no dream at all,
If I can sing the people's sorrow.

ABDUREHIM ÖTKÜR (1923–95)
TRANSLATED BY NICHOLAS KONTOVAS
AND EDITED BY GÜLNISA NAZAROVA

TRACES

We were children when we set out on this journey;
Now our grandchildren ride horses.

We were just a few when we set out on this arduous
    journey;
Now we're a large caravan leaving traces in the
    desert.

We leave our traces scattered in the desert dunes'
    valleys
Where many of our heroes lie buried in sandy graves.

But don't say they were abandoned: amid the cedars
Their resting places are decorated by springtime
    flowers!

We left the tracks, the station . . . the crowds recede in
    the distance;
The wind blows, the sand swirls, but here our
    indelible trace remains.

The caravan continues, we and our horses become
    thin,
But our great-grandchildren will one day rediscover
    those traces.

114   ABDUREHIM ÖTKÜR (1923–95)
TRANSLATED BY MICHAEL R. BURCH

WASTE, YOU TRAITORS, WASTE

Waste it all, you traitors, waste it, waste the bounty of
    this land,
And finally when that is not enough, then take its soul
    and waste it too.

Waste it to buy your king eyeshadow, waste it to buy
    your lord a belt,
Waste the only piece of bread that is left from all their
    pillaging.

Fine the farmer for his pasture, fine the shopkeeper
    for his simple cloth
A hundred times over, then take their blood to drink
    and waste it too!

See all the fish that fill its lakes, see all the wealth
    that is beneath it
And every step, a thousand times open a mine and
    waste that too!

Say 'What's-his-name is a so-and-so, and that Ötkür
    is such a thug'.
Break this nation into pieces, sell it off and waste its
    will.

ABDUREHIM ÖTKÜR (1923−95)
TRANSLATED BY NICHOLAS KONTOVAS
AND EDITED BY GÜLNISA NAZAROVA

MY FEELINGS

The light sinking through the ice and snow,
The hollyhock blossoms reddening the hills like blood,
The proud peaks revealing their breasts to the stars,
The morning-glories embroidering the earth's greenery,
Are not light,
Not hollyhocks,
Not peaks,
Not morning-glories;
They are my feelings.

The tears washing the mothers' wizened faces,
The flower-like smiles suddenly brightening the girls'
        visages,
The hair turning white before age thirty,
The night which longs for light despite the sun's
        laughter,
Are not tears,
Not smiles,
Not hair,
Not night;
They are my nomadic feelings.

Now turning all my sorrow to passion,
Bequeathing to my people all my griefs and joys,
Scattering my excitement like flowers festooning fields,
I harvest all these, then tenderly glean my poem.

Therefore the world is this poem of mine,
And my poem is the world itself.

WHEN WE CROSSED ILI

Why did tears gather in your eyes,
Today, my friend, as we crossed Ili?
Why did you recall those joyful memories,
As we awaited happiness as wide as that river?

Stop the car for a moment, you said,
Let's drink a glass from its edge!
Becoming one with the melodies of Ili,
Let's wade along Mother River's waters.

Stop, you said, halting our laughter,
You stood a while with your head bent.
You shed your tears on the River's pure breast
Like a child crying on its mother's lap.
Then, you said:

'This is not water that is flowing,
It is the tears of our families, their sighs.
And this is not a simple bridge, brothers,
This is where suffering transforms into blessing.'

We watched two fates, two worlds,
As we crossed the Ili River today.
Conflicting emotions overwhelmed us –
Destiny can split a person in half.

DOLQUN YASIN (1938–2005)   117
TRANSLATED BY MUNAWWAR ABDULLA

I AM A FRAGILE LEAF

I am a fragile leaf that trembled, then became still
My heart is full of pain and cannot beat freely
Because of your unfortunate fate, my love
I witnessed the anguish of your youth.

I grew slowly to the age of fifteen
While the storm clouds covered the sky
With open arms we welcomed the foe
A cowardly, ruthless oppressor crushed our hearts.

It's time to wake up, my love, our enemies are fierce
If you don't wake up, this age will make you weep
This age has made my face turn sallow
Now I am leaving, you remain in peace.

118   TURGHUN ALMAS (1924–2001)
TRANSLATED BY AZIZ ISA ELKUN

REMEMBERING

I don't know why I kept dreaming of you
I saw you very often in my dreams at dawn
You were beautiful as a flower in your youth
Even forty years on I remember your beauty still.

When I woke up, it came back to my memory
The image of you from those distant years
Whenever I remember you, my darling
You enter like fire into my soul.

On the day before I left, I prepared my horse
You stood there in tears, staring at me
After that, a mist came down
I could not see you, and I was full of rage.

Unexpectedly, we finally met again
The silver-white frost covering your hair
But I can see the frostiness on your face
I don't know whether it's a sign of joy.

January 1984

TURGHUN ALMAS (1924—2001)
TRANSLATED BY AZIZ ISA ELKUN

CONTEMPORARY
POEMS

NEVERENDING SONG

Every evening I sing a song,
Never able to stray from that street.
I eye a spot and I walk to it,
And, never reaching it, I get upset.
This evening I was passing by again,
Hammering the windows with a song,
When from somewhere a door squeaked open,
And an old man came out, scolding me:
'Are you crazy, you good-for-nothing,
Screaming like that every evening?
Yeesh, you won't let a man get some rest,
What sort of neverending song is this?'

'Do not scold me, old man,
You were once
Young, unable to sleep!
You too would sing, unable to stop,
Such a neverending song as this.'

TÉYIPJAN ÉLIYOW (1930–89)
TRANSLATED BY NICHOLAS KONTOVAS
AND EDITED BY GÜLNISA NAZAROVA

I COULD NOT FEEL

This life is a liar
I could not feel when it started
Or when it would end.
I could not even feel
The evergreen garden of my youth filling with
    autumn leaves.

When troubles came to me in life
I could not feel it when my hair turned white
I could not feel how I had abandoned my dreams
I was led astray by distractions.

While I was searching for love
I could not sense how my wings had tired
This world is a very mysterious place
I did not know what was true
and what was false.

124   MAHMUT ABDURAHMANOV (1934–2013)
TRANSLATED BY AZIZ ISA ELKUN

THE WRETCHED FATE OF THE UYGHURS

In spite of having an immense Motherland
My Uyghurs, you are scattered all over the world
No options remain but to hope for a better fate
But my Uyghurs, your fate will always be held in
    dispute.

After myriad migrations, you are still exiled from
    your homeland
You must not give up hope for your Motherland
Regardless of the difficulties and challenges you face
This burning homesickness shall never be doused in
    your souls.

Because of our wretched fate, we have all become
    refugees
But great hope remains in the souls of the next
    generation
Uyghurs across the diaspora are desperate
We are moths drawn to the fire of our homeland.

MAHMUT ABDURAHMANOV (1934–2013)   125
TRANSLATED BY AZIZ ISA ELKUN

MY STAR

As I pass border after border, mountain after
    mountain,
You stay in my heart, my love, with each step and
    each moment.

In my life you are the liberating star,
I chose my fortune, I said, and I looked to you.

As you shine as a guarantor for my hopes,
I am immersed in your river of love.

Oh, destiny! The clouds have obscured your light,
I have strayed from my path and grieved in the dark
    night.

Like Majnun I crossed the deserts of parting,
Reciting your name, I have crested so many hills.

When I mention you, my tongue is cut by the enemy,
While deep in my heart I sing odes to you.

A spark is entombed in a layer of the heart,
I've tried to shield it from the cruelty of winter.

My star, when you shine will you spill forth your
    light?
I await you wide awake every night.

Will this energy persevere in my heart,
Or has this agony of love been in vain?

126   AHMET IGAMBERDI (BORN 1937)
      TRANSLATED BY MUNAWWAR ABDULLA

HEROINE IN THE BLUE SHIRT
Dedicated to the unknown heroine of 5 July 2009[*]

What could your name be, oh beauty?
I know not and I am surprised –
Your name must be Mayimkhan, or Rizwan,
Nuzugum, or Iparkhan,[†]
Although the enemy tries to obscure it.

But your name is a thousand epics,
Heroine in the blue shirt!
Though I know not your name,
I decided to write your fame.
Defending your honour from humiliation,
Commanding the people's admiration,
You gave your precious life,
Heroine in the blue shirt!

You are bright, I say, as a star,
Rich of faith, grand you are,
Of perfect appearance, you are complete,
Blessed as the Heavenly Mountain's peaks,
Heroine in the blue shirt!

When the enemy blocked your path,
To your left and to your right,
Without bending your formidable height,
Your hand became a spear,
You spoke your words with courage,
Heroine in the blue shirt!

'Leave my land,' you said,
'This place has been ours from ancient times,
This pinch of earth is from my body,
These river waters are from my blood –
All the rest is from my life!'
Bravery rained from your tongue,
Heroine in the blue shirt!

You are my bright universe,
My lion-hearted heroine,
You are my sharp and fearless tongue,
You are the pride of this age.
My successor, daughter of Uyghurs,
Heroine in the blue shirt!

Adelaide, Australia, December 2010

* On 5 July 2009 a protest broke out in Urumchi following the
wrongful deaths of Uyghurs in the Chinese city of Shaoguan,
Guangdong province. The police and army cracked down hard
on the protesters, leading to 'riots', many deaths, and wide-
scale police sweeps after which many Uyghurs, particularly
men, disappeared. Over the next few days, women came out
to protest, demanding to know the whereabouts of family
members. On 7 July an iconic photograph showed a young
woman wearing a blue shirt confronting soldiers in front of
the tanks. No one knows her name or where she is now, but the
image lives on as a symbol of the bravery of the protesters.

✝ These are the names of well-known Uyghur heroines.

I SEARCHED FOR YOU

I searched for you
Like a desert which deserves silvery water.

I searched for you
Like a lake which fell in love with a swan.

I searched for you
Like a mountain for a white cloud.

I searched for you
Like a garden in the absence of a cuckoo.

I searched for you
Like a spring which desires a fountain.

I searched for you
At last, I found you, now don't go away.

ILYA BEKHTIYA (1932–87)
TRANSLATED BY AZIZ ISA ELKUN

THE UYGHURS ARE LIKE THIS

They dedicate all their savings to a wedding
They welcome their guests, giving everything away
If you say you don't understand – 'How can this be?'
You should know that the Uyghurs are like this.

Uyghurs' hands are skilful, their souls are like flowers
They transform their desert into orchards
They are faithful to their friends, their souls are pure
You should know that the Uyghurs are like this.

Uyghurs were put on this earth for good
Their knowledge spread to the wider world
If you ask with amazement, 'How can this be?'
– Because the Uyghurs are civilized like this.

They can't live without song and music and meshrep*
If you don't smile, they will not smile back
If you show respect, they will do anything for you
If you fell over, they would be ready to die for you.

---

* The Uyghur meshrep is a community gathering encompassing
music, dance, drama, poetry recital, story-telling and education.
This traditional event fosters a collective sense of unity and
solidarity and celebrates the richness of Uyghur culture.
Unfortunately, recent years have witnessed a distressing decline
in the frequency and freedom of these gatherings, as a result of
the severely repressive policies of the Chinese government in
East Turkistan. Nevertheless, the Uyghur meshrep stands as
a powerful symbol of Uyghur pride and resilience. It is worth
noting that in 2010 the Uyghur meshrep was inscribed on the
UNESCO List of Intangible Cultural Heritage, in recognition of
its vital contribution to global cultural diversity.

ILYA BEKHTIYA (1932–87)
      TRANSLATED BY AZIZ ISA ELKUN

LONGING

Will the spring arrive if you don't come?
Will the heart acquiesce should I not see you?
If you come and go once in a month or a year,
Will the heart be sated by such encounters?

A swallow came but you did not,
It came singing just like you.
And so salt tears come to my eyes,
Or did your heart turn away from me?

Whirl, become the wind and come,
Shake down an apricot for me and come.
Sure, make me sob and come,
Did the lover I miss spend the night on the road?

The orchard's eyes look your way,
Hold flowers in your hands and come.
If I lie in a corner alone without you,
Will my lover not be wronged?

Do you not know that I miss you?
Are you not aware that I cry?
Will you take my life away from me?
Can life remain in this body?

MUHEMMETJAN RASHIDIN (1940–2021)   131
TRANSLATED BY MUNAWWAR ABDULLA

YOUR LETTER ARRIVED, BUT YOU DID NOT

Your letter arrived, but you did not.
Who were they, that blocked your way?
How will I live if the enemy captures
Your hands before I can hold them?

Your letter arrived, but you did not.
At what inn overnight did you stay?
Will I not cry alone in the gardens
If you don't come when spring appears?

Your letter arrived, but you did not.
Are there rivers barring your way?
Is this the fate of lovers since the dawn of time?
Or is my lover's road really so impassable?

PEOPLE ARE WONDERFUL

Of days there are many types,
Of flowers there are many types.
My heart, don't be frustrated by people,
There are some who are excellent, too.

One may give bread to a beggar,
Another may give seed to the pigeons,
Another, if needed, will give his blood,
There are those who give their lives, too.

There are healthy people who may fall ill,
There are travellers who may become still.
If a country goes, there are kings, as well
Who end up gathering wood on a hill.

The world is marvellous, the people wonderful,
People themselves are banners for living,
Water for flames, embers for bleak winters.
That is why there are beautiful horizons.

Ghulja, 2 November 2000

MUHEMMETJAN RASHIDIN (1940–2021)   133
TRANSLATED BY MUNAWWAR ABDULLA

LONG LIVE

Long live those who help the helpless,
Long live those who clothe the naked.
Long live those who, when the sky rains jewels
Take none for themselves, and pray for rain.

Long live those who pay their father's debts
With the plane tree and its nourishing shade.
Long live those who, when their mother's cart horse
    tires
Become the horse and take the reins themselves.

Long live those who forgo their own comfort
And suffer for the happiness of others.
Long live those who blow upon the hearth
Of the lonely man whose fire has just gone out.

Long live those who light the torch and stay
Beside the wretched, in their lowly state.
Long live those who yield not to deception
When sometimes demons far outnumber angels.

Long live those who through love's myriad trials
Do not put their love of money first.
Long live those who do not burn to ash
Amid the glowing embers of worldly grief.

Long live those who, when friends praise you,
Do not belittle your worth or contribution.
Long live those whose hopes will never die,
Who will not let those passed be lost in dreams.

MUHEMMETJAN RASHIDIN (1940–2021)
TRANSLATED BY NICHOLAS KONTOVAS
AND EDITED BY GÜLNISA NAZAROVA

ON THE BANK OF THE RIVER DANUBE

Great River Danube, your waters are choppy.
Now I stand on your bank, do you recognize me?
Have you yet asked who I might be?
Did you ask heroic Attila who crossed you once?

Here I come today to visit you, bringing with me
    great longing –
There is no way I would give up my desires –
Because this awful thirst still torments me,
Because I cannot drink the wine of liberty.

Do you recognize me by my embroidered hat?
I am Uyghur but I don't have a flag at the UN –
Yes, I have a country but not an independent state!
And so I have no status in the world.

The Huns are no strangers to the Uyghurs,
But our lives are tasteless and lacking freedom
We are under the yoke of dictatorship
And for a long time Uyghurs have had no joy.

Do you recognize me by my embroidered hat?
The Huns and the Uyghurs spread from the same
    father
And the world once witnessed the lands
From Orkhun to the Tarim in our hands.

Without asking consent I drink your water from my
      hands –
We are brothers created by God.
When I see your blue smiling eyes
My heart is sad and my tears flow . . .

Budapest, 21 February 2011

AN ENTREATY

If I became the first minister of our God
The Uyghurs would be granted their own kingdom
If He commanded us to offer up our prayers for this
I would sacrifice my fortunes in this world and the
     next.

You gave land to my people but didn't grant us a
     country
Please swear that you will bestow one upon us
Endow the coming generations with strength and
     courage
Reward us with prosperity, wisdom and light
Give us the chance to ride
On the blue stone of good fortune
Grant us this; it is just the tip of a blade.

Let us be hopeful that God will answer our prayers
That you will know whether I am telling the truth or
     a lie.

Paradise will not be your homeland
Rather, your homeland is paradise!

ALMASBEK (BORN 1943)   137
TRANSLATED BY AZIZ ISA ELKUN

MISSING

Beauty never leaves my dreams
Her shining eyes filled with sadness and sorrow
When separation invades my soul
Now I am imprisoned, and she is in far-off exile.

Everything has gone, but it will never be forgotten
The love that once consumed you completely
That portrait of love will never let you have peace
How does my heart beat, even while it is bleeding?

Beauty that never leaves my dreams!

138   ALMASBEK (BORN 1943)
        TRANSLATED BY AZIZ ISA ELKUN

EVERYTHING REMAINS THE SAME

The beach we walked along whilst holding hands
The full moon we admired remain the same
The blue sea and even the green leaves
And the flowers in the valley are still the same.

The snow-covered mountain-tops and the lambs
The birds that flew together are still the same
But just one thing has changed, your soul
The land is green, but the tears remain the same.

ZEYNURE ISA (1941–2022)
TRANSLATED BY AZIZ ISA ELKUN

AFTER WORK

The Earth was our stage
and the moon was our spotlight.
We danced with joy
and our feet left beautiful traces
on the surface of the warm sand.
Love for the holy land entered through the soles of my
    feet.
It flows freely
Like thousands of suns through my veins.

GREETINGS TO MY HOMELAND

When I die
I wish to be able to rest
In the flower garden of my homeland
I wish to become the flagpole
Of a flag that we wave for freedom
I wish I could see my homeland
Without crossing the horizon's border.

THE STRUGGLE WILL NOT DIE

Without walking in the steps of the ancestors,
Without drawing the dagger in revenge,
Without my dreams having come to fruition,
Do not say that I have died, O people!

I have not died. I will not die. No, I will not die.

Without the blue flag flying over the homeland,
Without slaying the last of the enemy,
Without the dawn of freedom having broken,
Do not say that I have died, O people!

I have not died. I will not die. No, I will not die.

Without singing the march of victory,
Without this tyranny leaving my homeland,
Without the whole world knowing the Uyghur,
Do not say that I have died, O people!

I have not died. I will not die. No, I will not die.

I have not died. I will not die. The struggle will
    not die.

KÜRESH KÖSEN (1959–2006)
TRANSLATED BY NICHOLAS KONTOVAS
AND EDITED BY GÜLNISA NAZAROVA

OH, FATHERS!

All the poets speak of their mothers
Do you not remember your fathers?
They are such fathers
That even tigers might envy.

They are such fathers
That many beauties admired them
Their sharp knives ready to strike
If any betrayer should appear.

Always wading through water in boots
They have endured much suffering
They have drunk from horses' bits,
Crossed every mountain and plain.

At the tips of their spears, a bright star
On their swords, dawn's flame
Their love for their country shields them from arrows
Under their feet, waves of blood.

The slain lay in the desert
The sky wept down tears
Tamarind bushes welcomed them
Lions and tigers were their coffin-bearers.

We are known as dancing youths
Oh, fathers martyred in war.
We were grateful for needles
And forgot the arrows of battle
Our epics were written as staffs to lean on
But the sword created the world.

When mother gave me bread from the oven
My father fought in battle to give me freedom
Mother gave me a cotton shirt
Father gave me his battle flag.

When I fell down mother cried
Father picked me up and put me back on my horse
He trained me well to withstand hardship
So as not to be abused by my enemies.

In the shade mother sings a lullaby
In mother's arms I close my eyes
Father sings in the threshing ground
Like a king who has captured a city.

Conscience is calling my father
Mother is worrying about the family
The people's desires are a seething volcano
        in my father
He is a boat afloat on a river of tears.

The labour of a thousand youths
Traced in each callus on his hands
My every smile an endless debt
To the knife and bow he carried.

But now I am known as a party boy
Oh, dear father, you were martyred in battle.

THE CALL OF NUZUGUM*

Where are you, our heroic men?
Let us go to the desert,
The brave hunter finds freedom there,
It flows in his spirit and his blood.

The reeds sing a desert song,
Horses neigh on the horizon.
The heroic people who once lived by the sword
Now lie quiet beneath the earth.

The floating moon becomes a beautiful girl
Telling a story in the blue sky.
Oh, the reed-bed fiercely burns,
And with it the hopes of a whole nation.

We are listening to it silently,
Not only with our ears but in our hearts.
The sand encroaches on the fertile lands,
But we are the real sandstorms.

Let us go to the desert,
The delicate moon is telling a tale.
Perhaps there will be a book of warriors
Containing many beautiful myths.

It would not be strange to meet
Freedom's son, heroic Chin Tomur.
Let us live in a free world,
Singing desert songs all our lives.

* Nuzugum is an iconic heroine in recent Uyghur history.
During the rebellion against the Manchu-Qing Empire in
Kashgaria during the 1820s, along with thousands of other
people Nuzugum was forcibly moved to the Ili region. There
a Manchu military official forced her to marry him. On
the wedding day she killed the official and escaped to the
mountains. She survived for a month living in a cave until
Manchu soldiers discovered her and killed her by setting
fire to the reeds which surrounded her cave. Since then
Nuzugum's story has become a popular Uyghur legend, and
Nuzugum herself a nationalist symbol of resistance to foreign
invaders. Her tomb is situated in the Uyghur region of eastern
Kazakhstan.

FAITH

I have not given up faith in you yet
I am still waiting in that corner as you told me
Your every word feels like an arrow shot from a bow
Because our destiny has already been fixed
My life is dedicated to the moment when you
    remembered me
The light you ignited in my soul will never be
    extinguished.

I came alone to the road you once walked on
The echo stays deep inside me, never able to leave
The past has left us with deeply sweet memories
I will not venture to the cliff, nor will I meet you
We are apart now, as jealousy imprisoned us.

Urumchi, 14 October 2002

INFINITE LOVE FROM A HEART AS SMALL AS AN APPLE

A wine glass can be filled to the brim
But a river cannot flow in a brook
It is an undeniable ancient truth
And this saying endures in our people's hearts.

But my homeland, you are a different universe
You have gifted the incomparable feeling of love
I am a moth to you, you were placed in my soul
From a heart as small as an apple, my infinite love.

UYGHUR IMPRESSIONS

1. Loose Tobacco

Suspicious blood . . .
falls from a flower's mystery-stained face
into a palm where ears of wheat have died.

2. *Badam* Skullcap

Mourning a stallion scattered in eyelashes . . .
the stones that saw
ships flow from eyes
will turn to smoke.

3. Drum Dance

The wind of revelation
casts God to the dirt
when the call to prayer sounds in the body mosque.

4. *Muqam* Suite

Twelve fairies drag
a corpse
to their exquisite gardens.

5. *Etles* Cloth

Atop a rainbow
stretched from lust
to the sun of separation
I saw the grave that searches for my grandfather.

6. Thousand Buddha Caves

The suite of silence.
A castle
where the ogre of the soul lies captive.
The last descendant of the stone dynasty.

7. *Muselles* Wine

Angel of forgetting!
I'm your old friend, filled with memory moons.
Come, let's drink
from the skull of the celestial wolf.

8. Clay Oven

The wine chased out of the city
blooms in gold –
it is the mind we have forgotten.

9. Two-Stringed Lute

You
are a thorn-crowned song
leading caravans of golden camels
through the body wasteland.
I
am your third string.

10. Heart

Atop a glass cage
fell a dewdrop
with the world locked in its depths.

1991

EKHMETJAN OSMAN (BORN 1964)
TRANSLATED BY JOSHUA L. FREEMAN

MY LOVE

On this night's farthest continent I had you in my
      sight, my love,
your blood commanded soldiers and deprived me of
      the night, my love.

In the sky you feast with angels, on the battlefield
      I bleed,
the dusk of my lament brought you to earth from that
      great height, my love.

Shooting stars dripped endlessly onto the paper from
      my eyes,
yet still the body of the dark did grip my spirit tight,
      my love.

Always I've been a hunter, yet I've never come to
      know my prey,
you are the soul's gazelle, you stalk the hunter in his
      flight, my love.

You are Creation's mournful string, plucked by the
      finger of the light,
within my soul my passion is a sail that must unite,
      my love.

I kiss you like a grass of secrets grown in rivers of my
      flesh,
and from your lips flowed to my soul the blood of
      flowers bright, my love.

The wolf of life begins to howl each time I take you in
    my arms,
my corpse will be enveloped in the sky's great shroud
    of light, my love.

A dewdrop in my belly, you locked in your depths the
    world entire,
into the blessed wound you dripped, and there did life
    ignite, my love!

1991

EKHMETJAN OSMAN (BORN 1964)
TRANSLATED BY JOSHUA L. FREEMAN

NO ROAD HOME*

I have no lover's touch in this solitary corner,
I have no amulet for each night that brings me terror,
I have no thirst for anything but life,
With anguished thoughts in crushing silence, I am
    bereft of hope.

I don't know who I once was, what has become of me,
I don't know to whom I can speak of my heart's
    desires,
I cannot perceive the temper or nature of this destiny,
My love, I wish to go to you, but I am left bereft of
    strength.

I have seen the seasons change between the cracks
    and corners,
Yet all in vain, I receive no news from the blossoms
    and flowers,
This yearning pain has seeped right through to the
    marrow of my bones,
What is this place that I can journey to, but I have no
    road back home?

* This poem is believed to have been written by Abduqadir
Jalalidin from a prison cell during the current crackdown
which began in 2016.

THE HEART

Let's not blame life for being meaningless
One day loneliness will reach its peak
Even if we can't see how to achieve our desire
We can still shed silent tears.

Let's cry, maybe our tears will be beautiful
If they are shed silently for love
Even if we're always looking for bad luck
We're lucky when every night turns into a dream.

Let's not seek beauty only in the rose
The trace of blood on the thorn has beauty as well
When we contemplate the heart pumping blood
Its beating is just like the sweetest song.

PERHAT TURSUN (BORN 1969)   155
TRANSLATED BY AZIZ ISA ELKUN

THE TARIM RIVER

Just like the waters of the Tarim*
We began from here
And we will end here, in this land
We did not come from nowhere
And we will not go anywhere.

If God created humanity
Then God created us in this land
If humans descended from apes
Then we descended from the local apes.

Like a will that someone writes before death
Like blood that is dripping drop by drop
The Tarim river has many streams
We have a wound that has been open for ages
When will our blood congeal?

Sometimes we appear and disappear like the footsteps
    of a tribe
Occasionally we roar at the world like an imperial
    dynasty
But we have become extinguished
And the mountains howl like wolves
They howl to the whole universe about our
    disappearance
But nobody can understand their language.

The mighty angels and the God of light
Placed the Sun in the Sky as a flag.

When this era began
The rocky cliffs of mountains were painted with
    blood
And we climbed out from between the rocks
Now that the Sun had perished.

The sacred mountain has been taken away
By slowly moving stones one by one
This barrier was not able to save us
Only a single blood-soaked rose remains
The wanderer bows down
Before the power of Mother Umay[†]
Praying that disease will not infect him.

Beneath the glow of a bonfire abandoned by
    caravans
An azure flower secretly blooms
Don't we know our own bloodline?
It stretches down from the thousand-year-old
    mummies of the Tarim.
Check our origin; how did we get here?
Search for the shade of our skin in the dunes of
    the Taklimakan desert[‡]
Search for the source of our blood in the waters
    of the Tarim.

Just like the waters of the Tarim
We began in this place
And we will end here, in this land.

* The Tarim River is located in the south of the Uyghur homeland, and it is one of the longest endorheic rivers in the world. It ends in the Tarim Basin on the northern edge of the Taklimakan Desert.

✝ Umay is the goddess of fertility in Turkic mythology and Tengrism and is associated with women, mothers and children.

‡ The Taklimakan Desert is the second largest shifting sand desert in the world, located in the south-western Uyghur homeland.

TRANSLATED BY AZIZ ISA ELKUN

THE NIGHT

The darkness cannot light the street
The faint light shed by the stars is fading
Your melodies cannot melt my soul
Into your songs I sink like a piece of ice.

I wander the dark streets alone
Searching for a trace of that love
I feel that if love returns to this place
It will not embrace us again.

No need to shed tears for a dead love
These are raindrops that run down my cheeks
Perhaps if this rain falls one night
It will wash away my face . . . and everything.

PERHAT TURSUN (BORN 1969)
TRANSLATED BY AZIZ ISA ELKUN

ELEGY

'Your soul is the entire world.'
– Hermann Hesse, *Siddhartha*

Among the corpses frozen in exodus over the icy
    mountain pass, will you recognize me? Our
    brothers
we begged for shelter took our clothes. Pass by there
    even now and you will see our naked
corpses. When they force me to accept their massacre
    as love
Do you know that I am with you.

After three hundred years they awaken and do not
    know each other, their own greatness long
    forgotten.
I happily drank down poison, thinking it fine wine.
When they search the streets and cannot find my
    vanished figure
Do you know that I am with you.

In that tower built of skulls you'll find my skull as
    well.
They cut my head off just to test the sharpness of a
    sword. When before the sword
our beloved chain of cause and effect is ruined like a
    wild lover
Do you know that I am with you.

When in the market men with tall fur hats are used
     for target practice and a man's face draws out in
     agony as a bullet cleaves his brain, when
before the eyes that look to find the reason of their
     death the executioner fades and disappears,
reflected in that bullet-pierced brain's fevered
     thoughts will be my form, just then
Do you know that I am with you.

In those times when drinking wine was a greater
     crime than drinking blood, do you know the
     taste of the flour ground in the blood-turned
     mill? The wine
that Alishir Nava'i deliriously dreamed took its flavor
     from my blood.
In that endlessly mystical drunkenness's farthest,
     deepest chambers
Do you know that I am with you.

Xihongmen, Beijing, March 2006

MORNING FEELING

Every morning
the junk collector's harsh and ugly voice
through the cracks in the doors
through the cracks in the windows
with all its might presses into the house
Perhaps there's nothing sad about this voice
but with its harsh and ugly tone
it sounds so very sad to me

I recall
how many places
my address and phone number have been left
and with that I feel
that I've lost many things
I even sense I've lost
my deepest secrets
On broad streets
I feel stark naked
for no one comes to see me
and no one calls
Perhaps they hide somewhere and watch me
leering shamelessly at my phone number and address
as if leering nastily at my secrets

Not venturing outside
I sit here cursing them all
The junk collector's hoarse and ugly voice
the beauty of the sunlight on the buildings
the body odor rising from the blanket
all force one to admit
that the day has begun

Urumchi, 1993

NOTHING, THERE IS NOTHING ON THESE STREETS WITHOUT YOU

I cannot walk these streets without you
I cannot see the beauty of nature
I have crossed the streets many times, but you were
    never there
It seems there is no need to walk anymore.

Existence is miserable on these streets without you
The rain never ceases to call your name
All my existence has gone into following you
It seems I have left my sea shells on the beach.

As I wandered the streets without you
The wind suddenly asked, 'Who are you?'
I replied, 'It's not worth asking that question
I am nothing – there is nothing – on these streets
    without you.'

Haifa, 4 January 2016

THE CONFESSION OF A POEM

If you want to prohibit my speech
It would be better for you not to bother
If you find a way to block my mouth
I will find a way with my eyes.

And if you are going to blindfold me
My soul will simply rebel against it
My body will turn into words
The blood in my veins will explode.

If you do not let me utter the word 'right'
Then I will walk over to the right
If you block me from walking
Then I will fall onto my right side.

Increasingly I am becoming like air
It's possible to find me anywhere
It's utterly futile trying to stop me
Or attempting to rule or destroy me.

This is not a poem that stays inside a cage
It is more likely to be a lion
It's not a poem that you have killed
It is more likely to be a secret.

It would not be a poem if it were detained
It would not be a poem if it were killed
It is not a poem for blind people
It is only for those with quick eyes.

6 April 2013

ABLET ABDURISHIT BERQI (BORN 1971)
TRANSLATED BY AZIZ ISA ELKUN

AN ELEGY FOR MY HOMELAND

A bird
While it is inside a cage
Will not have to confine its thoughts and feelings
It's free and always will be.

When they earn their freedom
They are caged voluntarily
Their thoughts and feelings
Are locked inside a cage
Called their homeland.

27 December 2014

THE WORLD IN THE CITY OF KASHGAR

When the Sun greets the Uyghurs
When history greets the Uyghurs
The city of Kashgar becomes a fortress.

The stars gleam at dawn,
The seasons are flying through the trees,
The city soars through its legendary history
The people are here
With love in their hearts.

A horse-drawn cart
With a red sunshade
Passes me at dawn
Its bell jingling
With a basket on his head
A boy selling bagels
Passes me at dawn.

As I pass by a busy tea house
I don't let anyone know who I am
I am like a secret lover
Burning silently.

I look again and again
At every detail of the street
I kiss them quietly and lightly
I love
The white poplar trees in the daylight
Their silent shadows
Melting into one.

I love the rain that falls in September
It falls quietly on the water-slick road
The rain that cries in silence
Falls into the cracks of the mirror
The rain like pearls of light
I love my journey home from the mosque
The rain that falls from the hands of God.

Kashgar
The Idgah market is breathtaking
Uyghurs jostle against each other
The lovers who come to buy flowers
The blind who come to buy eyes
And the silent who come to buy rumours
Men buy bread in exchange for their lives
A woman sells herbs for dyeing eyebrows.

Young men stand by the fence
As if they were living in an unfamiliar city
They curiously observe everything, looking around
A naked infant runs into the middle of the road
The grown-ups begin to worry
They are frustrated, and ready to burn their clothes
In the imagination of a modernist poet
The human heart is like the sun
The minaret of the Idgah Mosque
Is like a heart
Pulsing anxiously.

You don't know
What your name is, or where your home is
Whether you exist in this world

You can only remember sleep.
Did you sleep for one night or for an hour
Or a century, or two centuries?
When you opened your eyes
The slanting rays of the sun shone
From the top of the minaret to the street
Placing your hands on the neck of such a lover
You feel like weeping.

No matter if you were in Paris
You would still feel that your smile did not belong
    to you
You would remember dampening your handkerchief
At least the pain you suffer in your country is
    your own
At least the tears that fall are in your mother tongue.

Despite drinking wine from a gold-plated cup
When foam floats to the top
You see in it the word 'homeland'
Every night in the Berlin sky
You see Uyghur eyes in every star
The holy church of Mary
Resembles the mosque that Uyghurs built
On the narrow street where you grew up
If one day you could go on a pilgrimage to Mecca
You would feel that God was left behind in your
    hometown
If your motherland is in hell
You will be a refugee forever in heaven.

My country, oh my country
Everything is so beautiful
And yet it's suffering as well.
The women of Kashgar
Live in a country built by men
They don't have an independent kingdom
But if they liked, they could bring it all down
Or they could make you a king
When they pour out their emotions
Their men become poets
They even win Nobel prizes
When they are unkind
Their wisdom turns to madness.

While I stand on this diminutive earth
I am a wave of the Tarim River
I wish to be able to flow into the sea
If I become a star in the dark sky of the Altai forest
I will shine for a Palestinian woman
And illuminate the grave of a prisoner.

I wish good luck for all in Jesus' language
I will carry a cross towards Jerusalem
Towards the young Jew
I am in the hottest of seasons of the Taklimakan
Reconciling the colour of the sand
And the green of Europe
I will cast smiles and become the weather
Of every corner of this vast world
I am a tiny spot casting light
On the map of the world.

The homeless birds
Cry for the seasons, calling for their homeland
While the wandering wind carries
Leaves of its own.

'BUT A THORN WAS LEFT IN OUR TONGUES . . .'

Blessing
Dedicated to A. I. Elkun

Finally, we met
First on the phone –
Then just as the dusk fell
A red taxi parked next to us
Leaving no trace of misery
But a thorn was left in our tongues.

Your blessing belongs in a foreign language
Your two daughters are as white as snow
And they feel no unease
They flew with an English spell
On their semi-transparent wings.

They have fallen
Into the Uyghur language –
The language that God blessed
The sky is covered over tightly
It seems everlasting but still our words reach their
      listeners.

The silence is swiftly deepening
Faster than the light
Shocked, I hold my tongue
I try not to mention the wild pigeon*
My notebook is erased in white
But my pen is louder than a bowstring . . .

A lamb is born in a stable
Grass grows in the stream
My fourth son will soon be born, and will emerge
Into the night where the moon and stars come out . . .

A bunch of black grapes
Hangs over the white paper
If you don't eat them, I will
Oh readers, the night is just one page long.

Urumchi, 27 August 2012

* Here the poet refers to 'The Wild Pigeon' ('Yawa kepter'), a
famous story by Nurmemet Yasin Orkishi. It is an allegorical
story of the son of a pigeon king who is trapped and caged by
humans while on a mission to find a new home for his flock.
The Chinese authorities considered it a criticism of their
government's presence in the Uyghur Region, and Nurmemet
was sentenced to ten years in prison.

ADIL TUNYAZ (BORN 1970)   173
TRANSLATED BY AZIZ ISA ELKUN

I WAS THAT PERSON

Floating on a wave of blood
Remaining in a courtyard of silence
Surrounded by the sound of darkness

I was buried by the indoctrinated words of oppression
I was behind a fallen wall
I was the umbrella underneath rain that fell like rocks
I was hopeless and hidden within a cart-driver's
    broken whip
I was the glistening red on the blade of a sword that
    pierced my body
I was walking with a spirit that was already dead.

From that moment, the hope embedded in the rocks
    began to melt in the rain
The person who walks on the path under the darkness
    of souls
I am the drop that falls from the willow trees on the
    riverbank
Were you aware that person was me
The human being who died and slowly began to
    dissolve?

Rain from the dark clouds in the sky falls on you
You empty your thoughts to the stars
Thorns and flowers grow in the footsteps you left.

From your tearful stare to your frozen stance
From dawn to dusk you relive the time when you were
    abused.

Candles which kept burning despite the ghostly winds
Rays of sunlight blocked by the devils' hands and torn
The beam of the sun which crushed the bones of the
    moon
A lonely tree which mourns its falling yellow leaves.

I am a tongue which speaks from the gentle wind that
    kisses your face
I am a sign of happiness you see before you close your
    eyes
Did you know I am the person who was forgotten by
    your lips?
I am in your veins, in your breath and your voice
I am in the corner watching from a ladder that
    reaches to the seventh floor
I am that person who shares the milk of regret with
    you.

RAHIM YASIN QAYNAMI (BORN 1975)   175
TRANSLATED BY AZIZ ISA ELKUN

AWAITING

I bathed my isolation in the sunshine
Destiny revealed itself in the silence
Where were you, my love, when my soul suffered?
I gently closed my eyes and wondered.

Who do you remember? Who were you waiting for?
It's clear that you are still alive in my heart
I thought you crossed a road in great haste
I was unable to think of anything but you.

The poplar trees gaze at me with sorrow
There is a realm of faith that shines as bright as you
My love, I am certain you will be able to survive
If suddenly a massacre occurs in this land.

I will always remember your mournful eyes
You must have left home aching for me
I have endured my life for another day
While waiting for you I have joined the stars.

TRANSLATED BY AZIZ ISA ELKUN

I FELT LIKE IT

I gazed at the blue sky
Touched the leaves
And listened to a beautiful song
Just because I felt like it . . .

I put sugar crystals into my tea
My tears fell into the garden
I looked down because I felt like it.

I watered flowers
I cleaned the ashtray
I dropped food into the lake
Because I felt like it.

The flying time reminds me of you
For me the mountain has shrunk to the ground
Love's thorny path has left no soul untouched
I feel like this.

Thinking of that place where you live, shedding
    my tears
Making my life worse at your desire
In this way I am becoming dried out
Feeling like this.

From what I know, life is like this, and it will never
    be enough
Death may also be like this; you cannot delay it
Poems are also like this; you should not write
Feeling like this.

Who can I love, when I feel like this?
Who can I set aflame, when I feel like this?
If we survive, can we meet again as before
Take a stroll with the person we love
While holding their hand?

CRY, WIND

Cry wind, for the leaves you have blown from
    the trees
Cry wind, for the wounds you have torn apart
Cry wind, for the forests you have stripped
I will learn to cry, to cry from you.

Cry wind, for the flowers, the lilacs you have scattered
Cry wind, for the rivers held still with blue ice
Cry wind, for the empty treeless courtyards
I will learn to cry, to cry from you.

Let the dark eyes that beheld my beloved be yours
Let the words of heartbreak I spoke to my beloved
    be yours
Cry wind, the bullet in your heart is mine
I will learn to cry, to cry from you.

Cry wind, for the anguish of stones and mountains
Cry wind, for the hopes and dreams of falcons
Cry wind, for the torments of lovers
I will learn to cry, to cry from you.

COLORFUL WORDS

In black you're fooling the white of death
You're rinsing green life's yellow waters
You're dyeing your days a boring red
You're speaking
of love's filthy disease
and even
of how your heart died of this disease
of how days past
march down dark roads holding torches
of how in the eternal smiles of the dead
as in God's face
all colors extinguish without a trace

CHRONICLE OF AN EXECUTION

A drop of sky from Paradise streams
A bud from the bonfires on Hell's branches
A bundle of black rocks in the heart
Grateful gifts for the verses that flow toward
     the moon
A page of the epics where heroes lie buried
The past that advances shouting Charge!
The odes sung by souls entering and leaving
to doors opening and doors closing
Distant graves drawing ever closer
Girls never seen twice and beds seen many times
Water in the blood, bread in the flesh, vows in
     the bone
A sword striking a head, a noose lain round a neck,
     bullets into the chest
And what comes before his eyes in the final breath
is a chain called homeland, an enemy called his people
And the beautiful life for which he longed
is the flower garden he has laid waste

GHOJIMUHEMMED MUHEMMED (1971–2018)   181
TRANSLATED BY JOSHUA L. FREEMAN

HISTORY

I paged through body bonfires
and saw the sky with an icebound sun.
I paged through desert dunes
and saw faith with withered roots.
I paged through rebellions of the soul
and saw Mashrab on a gallows hanged.

The city withdrew from the countryside,
threadbare stones lie cramped in the ravine,
rivers run silently between parched banks . . .
I took up a handful of soil
and my homeland bathed in my umbilical blood.
I took up a handful of sand
and just then horses neighed in my soul.
I opened my chest
and saw armor full of holes.
I took off the armor
and saw God sleeping on a porch.

I live in the city,
I bring home rivers and lakes,
I bottle and eat the trees.
I watched two people begging for change
on a ten-story building's front steps
and saw a caravan of riders in the Uyghur desert
struggling to mount their camels.

TRANSLATED BY JOSHUA L. FREEMAN

I OPENED MY DOOR

I opened my door
in hopes that a girl might come bearing flowers

I took off my clothes
to make sure she could recognize me

I removed the masks
from my two faces, white and black

I rubbed the colors from my smile
brushed the dust off of my sorrows
tore up
my poems that sang of eternal devotion

Sweeping away all the trash of my heart
I prepared myself to love

Khotan, October 2009

GHOJIMUHEMMED MUHEMMED (1971–2018)   183
TRANSLATED BY JOSHUA L. FREEMAN

FIRST NIGHT: AT SIX O'CLOCK

At six o'clock
On a day like a wild pomegranate
Yet again it enters quietly through the door
That busy-to-death-ness
It's consuming me with ecstasy
It's blossoming on my body like a flower.

It doesn't let me sleep.
It writes a poem about me.
It's a wound in the night.
It goes away along the street.
Like the wound inside me
Like the man in my dream
Like a beautiful woman
Or a screaming child.

At six o'clock
I enter by another door
I'm evaporating like water
I'm flowing like light
I'm soft as a cloud.

Then I return again, alone, with nothing left
These roads where snow fell last year
Will take me far away
At exactly six o'clock.

4 December 2015

GÜLNISA IMIN GÜLKHAN (BORN 1976)
TRANSLATED BY AZIZ ISA ELKUN

TENTH NIGHT: THE SUNLESS SKY

The women's prison
Smiles from under the snow
The women's prison
Emerges running at daybreak.
Dirty, cracked and bleeding hands
Marked on the surface of white snow
A map of the women's prison.

They don't want to shed their tears
They just want to lift their heads
They just want to gaze at the sunless sky.
Their troubles, their yearning
Their nightmares and sleepless nights
They want to talk about it with someone on the
      outside.

GÜLNISA IMIN GÜLKHAN (BORN 1976)
TRANSLATED BY AZIZ ISA ELKUN

NINETY-EIGHTH NIGHT:
A CURSED WOMAN

Women were madly loved
They were fiercely protected
They were exchanged for cities, countries and crowns
They were praised to the skies
The madness ran free
Women ran into the reeds to escape
Women gave birth inside caves
Women were hanged
They were locked inside exotic harems
Long hair on their severed heads
They rotted inside dungeons
They were kidnapped by brigands
Gifted to soldiers
They were killed a thousand times
Pierced by a thousand thorns
Women could have become anything
But they were persuaded by one word
Eve was a woman who was pursued
Eve was a woman who was expelled
Eve was a woman . . .

DREAMS OF YOU

You are in my dream
I hug you gently
I look into your eyes
There was snow falling on that day
There was a girl in a white dress.

She kisses you, tasting the honey from your lips.

I want to capture the depth of your soul
She can appear to you
She can fly to you like a windswept leaf
She can make a necklace with the beads of your
        distressed soul
She can hold your hand and lead you far away
To the place where the Earth meets the Sky.

We will have a home
We will live on our love
If you tell me to forget you
I will blush scarlet and look down
Will that day ever arrive?
Will this world let us embrace in kindness?

These dreams are mine
In these dreams you are also mine
If you hug me gently in your arms
Like snow in sunlight
I will melt
I will sink into the Earth.

Now it is eleven o'clock
I will close my eyes
To have more dreams of you.

188   RISALET MERDAN (BORN 1970)
TRANSLATED BY AZIZ ISA ELKUN

I AM WAITING FOR YOU

Quietly the door opened halfway
Then it stopped
I was expecting him to enter the room
I was looking outside through my window
There were many lives entering and exiting
The door kept squeaking, creaking as it opened
But I could not see anyone
I could only see a shadow.

I am waiting for you
You have to come soon
My door is open for you
Come in
Come like a gust of summer wind
Or
Like a shower of autumn rain.

RISALET MERDAN (BORN 1970)
TRANSLATED BY AZIZ ISA ELKUN

BITTER POMEGRANATE

You are a single pomegranate, as red as me,
You have laughed at life amongst your leaves.
You have sat on branches, immersed in thought,
Immersed in bitterness.

I bit into you and was left disappointed.
I don't want to curse you, or punish you,
Perhaps I, too, am a pomegranate in this life.
I felt like telling you quietly
Of the gloomy feelings inside me.

You are a bitter pomegranate,
But you are obsessed with a sweet emotion.
You are a bitter pomegranate,
Bringing tears to my eyes.
In life am I sweet or bitter?
I hadn't thought about it till now.
I am a single grain of sand, or a pomegranate,
A pomegranate seed in this still life.

Bitter pomegranate,
Slowly I loved you.
Thinking of myself as you,
I peeled off your rind, and threw it away.
Splay open for me, like this naked life.

TODAY IS A DAY TO WRITE POEMS

Today is overcast,
A sun blazes in my core nonetheless.
Today I have no inspiration,
Lines assemble one after the other.

Remember or forget me,
Life, I have thought of you always.
My fists are unclenched nonetheless,
I have no remorseful sighs in me.

Come and embrace me, Grief,
Today is a day to write poems.
Sleep won't come to these eyes tonight,
For this first step taken anew.
Today is a day to write poems,
Kissing resolution on the lips,
I've stopped expecting hope from anyone.
Today is a day to write poems,
Loving myself in silence.

RISALET MERDAN (BORN 1970)   191
TRANSLATED BY MUNAWWAR ABDULLA

RETURNING TO THE FIRE

I will return to him,
Return to them!
My eyes can't sleep anyway,
I see a night through all my days . . .
Down my fingers my stars are seeping away.
I will sit beside him and close my eyes,
Let the dark dungeons have their nightmares!
Let my dreams laugh by their side . . .

Never mind, let my hands be tied,
As long as it's not my heart being burned again.
Whips, please slash my face,
My strangled soul cannot take anymore,
The noose is about to break!

Don't cry if you hear the news of my 'passing'!
Say the cold, the hunger, the thirst,
And the crisis of identity
Set me free.
Cast the stones from your heart,
Don't give me another thought.

It is my hatred for sobbing that will buy the ticket,
It is my hatred for weeping that will pull my luggage,
It is the mourning, which seized my heart,
That will release my veins and relax my fears,
When the black bag over my head shouts, 'Urumchi',
It is just my burial shroud running for my mum's
       tomb . . .

What ease to go back like this!
With cruelty to grant my wishes,
Before the final death.

When you hear the strange news 'He died',
Say, 'He is not dead',
How can one die in the soil of one's homeland?
His only duty now is to smile,
Clinging to the bright white earth that has been his
home all the while.

8 February 2019

WRITTEN AND TRANSLATED BY
MUYESSER ABDUL'EHED (HENDAN) (BORN 1984)   193
EDITED BY DARREN BYLER

HE WAS TAKEN AWAY

On one of your mornings
on my high noon journey
on their seaside stroll at dusk
on the darkest dais of his night
he was taken away.

It seemed the sun was glaring at you,
a nightmare seemed to come upon me,
they seemed struck by thunder's omen.
Sleep seemed pulled out of his life
and he was taken away.

Now eyes will pierce our thresholds,
now no hearts will water the streets,
now no one will wash the shirts he takes off
like a mother washes a lost child's clothes.
Now time will not run,
it will walk heavy like a turtle
with love pushing from behind.
Now all means will fade in the distance
while an anxious woman searches
for barefoot children.
Now the world will learn sorrows with no cure,
now fingers will count themselves,
often the fingers will cut knives.

He was like me,
he could see.
He was like you,
he could read.

He was like them,
he could speak.
He was a man,
a man taken away,
with a crime the prisons wrote for him
as a doctor writes prescriptions.
On a paper written for his death
I will yellow,
you will blanche,
they will turn blue,
and we can never enter his color,
we will find no color like his color.

11 June 2020

AN EAR ON THE WALL

As soon as we arrived
Our parents convinced us the walls had ears.
It was only later that we realized everything else
    did, too.

The story was, as the elders said, mouths pressed
    to ears,
The youths we had played with growing up
Had vanished one night as if abducted by jinn.
They had been standing under a wall with ears.

Until the day we arrived in Sweden
We lived a thousand years every day surrounded
    by them.
No walls had ears here,
In fact, the people had none either.
You might try to tell them something
On the streets and squares with loudspeakers,
But no one would listen.

They did not believe that walls could have ears,
That there were ears around us.
But in the homes of Swedish Uyghurs
Every wall is covered with them.
Carrying ears inside themselves, they smuggled
    them in
From the country they had left.

If a person laughed, they looked angry.
If a person smiled, they looked sarcastic.
They believed the tea they drank and the food they
    ate had ears.
They were too anxious to dream, to think,
Because they had ears on themselves, too.

They could not live without them,
They did not believe the Swedish walls had none.
Unable to imagine an earless life,
Scared to death of standing below an earless wall,

They lived. Eventually,
Part of them became an ear on the wall.

ABDUSHUKUR MUHAMMET (BORN 1967)   197
TRANSLATED BY MUNAWWAR ABDULLA

MY NAME

I am Abdushukur Muhammet
but my name is a stranger to me,
draped over me like a spider's web.

Perhaps it had run away
from a land I had never visited
and found itself in the Taklimakan.

It's misspelled too
like the kiss of the wrong first love,
and too long
like my longing,
like my never-ending thoughts,
like my unverbalized anguish.

Sometimes it looks like the demolished mosques,
sometimes like the old grave my father bequeathed me,
and other times like the circular naan of Kucha.

Its twisting lines, like a state border
turn me
into the pair of elm trees at my father's grave.

My father was not the prophet
but we were chased from our country like the prophet
bearing the name Muhammet.

You are hung up on the wall of a forgotten museum,
worn away like stones by centuries of wind.
O museum, passed through by the living and settled
        by the dead,
O world, where truth and lies are one and the same,
in the bloodstains of those diseased eyes,
may names scar over in the colour of sand.

Bathe me with my name
when I die
if it still wants me.

ABDUSHUKUR MUHAMMET (BORN 1967)
TRANSLATED BY MUNAWWAR ABDULLA

A DAYDREAMER

I have become a daydreamer
I search for an air in my dream
My mother sings whilst rocking the cradle
Lullaby, lullaby, and kisses.

I have become a daydreamer
I search for a phrase in my dream
My father taught me when I started to speak
Defend your homeland; treat it like your own eyes.

I have become a daydreamer
I search for a path in my dream
Well-trodden by herdsmen driving sheep
My knees sink deep into the dust.

I have become a daydreamer
I come to a cave in my dream
When I collapse, feverish for love
The lover in my heart brings me water.

I have become a daydreamer
I search for a place in my dream
Where I sang during Ramadan's nights
A companion of the crescent moon.

I have become a daydreamer
I search for a road in my dream
Where I met a long-bearded elderly man
Who wished me well and said 'Stay safe'.

I have become a daydreamer
I see a bird fly in my dream
It cries and implores 'Take me with you'
It flutters and lands in its nest.

OMER IMIN (BORN 1967)
TRANSLATED BY AZIZ ISA ELKUN

KAMAL HAS GONE

On December 18th, I was on the train
I thought I heard someone calling my name
'Yes,' I replied, surprised.
In front of my seat
An elderly man was sitting
He pointed to the window with his cane
Snow was falling
It melted as soon as it touched the ground
Why does snow not have eyes?
Why does it not fall onto the roofs of houses,
Or on leaves
The sea, and the fields?

On that particular day of the first snowfall
Before the world could see
Before a woman could smile
Kamal had gone.

Kamal had gone
It passed midnight
I miss you
Because I miss you, I fall like rain.

It was the last time
Not long before you went
One of your sayings that I will always remember
'My daughter, you must stand firmly on the ground,
and remember me without crying.'

Kamal has gone
But still he has not left me
I loved him for fifty years
And it was not enough.

Yes, I will stand firmly on the ground
I will remember you without tears
I will see your eyes when I look at my own
I will remember your poetic words
I will remember your face that disappeared into the
    light.

Our phones silent since 2018
The accompanying fear and frustration
And a burning melancholic homesickness
On that day, December 18th, when the snow first fell
You called my name
You looked for my presence
I will always remember that day.

RAHILE KAMAL (BORN 1968)   203
TRANSLATED BY AZIZ ISA ELKUN

LET THE BIRDS SING

The birds are singing a melody of spring,
The scent of spring gives me the utmost joy.
My bird, keep on singing for freedom,
I'm sorry if I frightened you.

The sound of your song is truly amazing,
Your subtle melody entrances me.
My bird, keep on singing for freedom,
Be my friend and soulmate.

A DESCRIPTION OF LIGHT

Tonight is mine
Your footsteps closing in on me are mine
Dreams of every moment are likewise mine
The shadow which approaches me is mine
The breath that you are drawing in is mine
Your fingers which are keen to link are mine
The sounds that flow towards my heart are mine
To have tea with you is my joy
'Goodbye, to my incomparable joy'
The tranquillity you have brought me is solely
    mine, but
The beautiful existence of the distance
That remains between us is not mine.

ABIDE ABBAS NESIRIDIN (BORN 1992)   205
TRANSLATED BY AZIZ ISA ELKUN

ON THE BOAT

The blue sea rolls constantly
there is nothing but water
and seagulls
fish . . . and other lives
but they can't capture my soul.

Though a shark is swimming inside my house
You are worrying about your homeland.

Why aren't you like the others?
You can't laugh from your heart.

When you mention your homeland
Your body starts to tremble,
Even though my homeland
Now only lives in my dreams . . .

I stared at the sea, torn asunder.
The sea turned out to be a tear in my eyes.
Oh Taklimakan, Taklimakan,
You are flowing with my tears.

ABDUREHIM PARACH (BORN 1974)
TRANSLATED BY AZIZ ISA ELKUN

THE VANISHED SKY

Within the icy snow of dark winter
Stand Uyghurs' houses
Martyrs are lying without burial cloths
They look like scattered pomegranate seeds.

The sky hides itself
Inside the shooting stars.

BEING LATE

Look at the bright day
And the night's blue hue.

Look
Spring arrived late
Just as you once said
'I will come back soon'
Just like the promises you made.
We have been waiting too long
So long that our souls have started to bleed.

The seasons do not repeat themselves here
Not because our eyes are tired
But because our souls are.

The longing continues
The waiting seems never-ending
Until you return from the East
Or I come to you.

THE MONUMENT OF BETRAYAL

Inside my traumatized body
The light passing through refracts
While searching for light, I approach myself
The sweet pain of harsh separation chokes me.

While I am searching deep inside myself
I receive a pair of mourners from the spirit of hope
I buried the unknown deep inside my soul
It is the world that has betrayed me.

If I could murder myself
Oh, I would not cry for you at night
If I didn't betray myself
I wouldn't swear at my heart which has become
    a stone.

My nights are filled with regret
I have built a bloodstained monument within my soul.

ALIMJAN METQASIM GHEMNAKI (BORN 1992)   209
TRANSLATED BY AZIZ ISA ELKUN

RESURRECTION

The screaming sound
Of a man who belongs to the deep night
A widow is whispering to the wall
People who have lost their hope
At that moment
Are all resurrected before my eyes.

COMMON NIGHT

This is a night made from words.
This is a night poured like cast iron into our spines.
This is a night that lodges us in slippers and in the
    bedrooms we keep within books.
This is a night that makes our noses shed hellfruit
    leaves.
This is a night for us to make merry with lovers in
    illusory castles.
This is a spring night that softly grasses our daily
    footprints on prayer rugs and constantly weighs
    down our eyes.
This is a celestial night that makes the promising into
    the probable.
This is a mother night that suckles death verses.
This is a night that no elegy, ode, rain, or beam of
    light shall ever reach.
This is a hungry night,
this is a naked night.
This is a night far from Satan and from God.
This is a night that calls to mind
the darkness of the womb
the vague cries of infancy
the solo games of adolescence
the first love of youth
the sudden futility of adulthood
the grim dusk of old age
the terror before death.
This is a night that patiently waits
to seep from our pores

and seize our whole body
as we cast off from shore.
This night is a sky for all buildings, shadows,
   traditions, betrayals, revolutions, mattresses,
   bats, novels, songs, pictures, journeys, murders,
   and smokable substances.
This night is ink to all pens.
This night is bosom to all secrets.
This night is the Antichrist whose tongue drags along
   the land of history.
This night is the mud that sticks to our shoes as we
   walk in the forest of meaning.
This is a night that shatters Noah's ship and makes
   traps of its decks.
This is a night that takes all we have, hands it over to
   the only one who speaks, and quietly walks on.

'THE THIRD'

Mother cut her own umbilical cord
She didn't tell anyone the news or celebrate
Father called an adhan in fear
That morning they gave a name to their baby.

A secret joy, the baby to her is everything
She keeps her child concealed from others' eyes
A changeling child without a role or rights*
She opened her eyes in fear at being born.

The three siblings cannot walk together
Or leave their home and play outside,
'The third' child had no right to be born
Hiding in a corner is the only game she knows.

They have a strange set of rules for giving birth
The 'third' child has to live secretly
It is a routine affair for the cruel oppressor
To tear children away from their parents' arms.

The youngest child has learned
To hide under the bedding when strangers come
The unfortunate family has to keep the secret
While loving and caring for their 'third'.

Mother is sorrowful but hoping
For light to come in through the window
When will 'the third' child be freed from this secrecy
And be able to live the life of a child?

* This poem was inspired by Kazakhstan-based Uyghur artist
Gülnaz Tursun's 16 October 2017 painting, 'The Third'. It
refers to the strict birth-control policy implemented in China
since the 1980s, according to which families were legally
permitted only two children. Any subsequent children were
deemed illegal, and the family would be subject to heavy
fines if they were discovered by the authorities. Although the
policy has now been abandoned in Inner China, it has been
implemented even more strictly in the Uyghur region since
2017, with widespread reports of the forced sterilization of
Uyghur women.

MOTHER EARTH, YOU ARE MY HOLY LAND

Wherever I go, I see unfamiliar faces,
But they all smile cheerfully
And they all go by, diffusing their fragrance.
Mother Earth, you are my Holy Land.

The silvery water flows in narrow streams,
Cascading from the snowy peaks of mountains
Where white swans swim in the lakes.
Mother Earth, you are my Holy Land.

The leaves whisper and rustle in revelry,
A gust of wind blows from the wilderness
And you can hear the branches singing.
Mother Earth, you are my Holy Land.

TUYGHUN ABDUWELI (BORN 1974)   215
TRANSLATED BY AZIZ ISA ELKUN

THE WORLD

The world is cast before my eyes
But its smile is disagreeable
It looks like an injured lion
It's agitated and roars with fear.

The world is cast before my eyes
My glass of wine is full
But it will be drunk by another
That's probably the destiny of life.

DO NOT LET YOUR HEART BURN, MOTHER

Crying for me too long, you have lost your voice
The devil of cruelty has made your eyes red with tears
My calm spirit will resist this agony forever
Do not let your heart burn, mother
You should have passed it to me, instead
I would have let myself burn like logs.
Do not let yourself shatter
Do not let yourself endure these torments
Pray for your son and give him the chance to die
        for you
For his dear mother's happiness.

ABDUWELI AYUP (BORN 1973)   217
TRANSLATED BY SUBI

MIHRAY*
Obituary

Mihray,
When you were delivered
I was sixteen years old
You were the first new life I ever held
It was good news when I was told
Our family rejoiced
The world was alive that day
The moon was full and bright.

The moon was smiling from the window
Shining in the dark
I called you Mihray
It means 'love for the moon'.

You were the life I held in my arms
You were the spirit
That made me feel warm
Your innocent eyes
Your bright smile
All brought me happiness.

The cold iron cage I was trapped in
Also grabbed you so tight
And squeezed you
Squeezed you to death.

Rain is falling, trickling down my arm
The rain is wearing away a hole
In my mind
The clouds are crying, but my lips are dry
     like a desert
Rain is wearing away a hole in my heart
And the emptiness is dry, so dry.

The hole in my heart is empty
Like a well dug in the desert
How can my eyes shed so many tears?
When will my eyes be dry?

* 'Mihray' was written by Abduweli for his niece, who died
in a Chinese concentration camp in late 2020. Mihray was a
talented biotechnologist at Tokyo University. She was arrested
after returning to Kashgar, her hometown, to visit her parents
in August 2019. Mihray was thirty-one years old when she
died.

WE HAVE NOT MET

It's a strange secret
Because we haven't met
Our breath has yet to collide
The heat of our hands has yet to combine.

We've never met
But we have connected implicitly
It is, indeed, a strange secret.

We never went to the park
Nor sat on a park bench
We never left any traces behind
There was no forest we could walk in
We have no stories to tell for the long nights
Yes, it's a strange kind of secret.

I desired your love
But you are tired of being loved
We look at each other from afar
We use our love as a shield
It's a strange love, and secret.

IF YOU FORGET ME

The Sun will not smile on you
A storm will enter your life
My teardrops will hit your windows like rain
You may say farewell to the spring
If you forget me.

When regret takes over
Does wind blow dust inside you?
Does your body shiver like leaves?
Will you no longer have untroubled dreams?
You may have a peaceful soul
But even if you forget me
The flame of my love will continue to burn
      within you.

AYGUL ALIM (TAMCHE) (BORN 1979)
TRANSLATED BY AZIZ ISA ELKUN

VERSES OF FALLING

The hopes that had begun to smile, have just
    committed suicide.

The wailing wind and murky road
Stand between me and my love
I catch everything at the moment of despair
Anyway, we will all disappear one day
We will melt on the streets of love where we once
    desired
We will go on walking as if nothing has happened
And our walks will go on walking by themselves
As if nothing has happened to us.

I visited that street again
It was covered in fog like before
Doubt is lying there
I have nothing with me except my loneliness
It was tempting to escape, to leave the sorrow
Or the sadness that may begin to pay rent, but . . .
Or the sadness that has been taken up by rent, but . . .

I don't know why
We were both on this path
Usually no one walks this way
No one walks this way except people who have been
    abandoned

I have not abandoned myself
But my self has abandoned me
It threw me away in a far-off land.

I write this poem now
Because I forget poetry when I am happy
I devote every word of these verses to trauma.

IHSAN ISMAYIL (UMUN) (BORN 1994)   223
TRANSLATED BY AZIZ ISA ELKUN

LET'S MIGRATE, DARLING

If the reality that we dream of
Is smashed by the betrayal of truth
Then come to me, my darling
And let's sink into the petals.

Let's spread our spirit
Open the doors to love
Let's migrate
Towards the country of light.

Flowers have bloomed from our love
Water has been cleansed by our adoration
Footsteps that we left with and loved
Have gone to the safekeeping of God.

Come to me, my darling
Let's migrate
Like candles, we were born to burn
Let's fly away.

GIFT OF THE SKY

Like dew under the sunlight
My love, your eyes are shining
Like a fairy walking in paradise
You open the door of my feelings.

I am touched by your mystery
Your charming glance melts my soul
Just as the morning breeze, escaping after a kiss
Suddenly wakes my somnolent mood.

A beautiful smile on your face
Reflecting your pure soul like a mirror
Even though the journey of life is not straight
One day the bird of fortune will land on you.

The scent of pure winter in your hair
Your eyebrows like the wings of the swallow
In your heart there is so much sunshine
Your lips await the joy of love.

All the beauties belong to you
You are given to the poet as a gift of the sky
My soul burns with emotion like fire
You inspire me to write an epic.

VILYAM MOLUT (BORN 1974) 225
TRANSLATED BY AZIZ ISA ELKUN

TO SEE

When I look at the Sky
All existence has a fiery hue
When I look at the Earth
Everywhere is covered with water.

The Sky heaves a sigh of exhaustion
The Earth feels a sense of great sorrow
When I observe myself closely
I can see you in my eye.

A MIRACLE ARTIST

I told myself, let me try being an artist
I painted the sun, but it could not shine
I painted the stars, but they could not twinkle
I painted the sea, but it could not swell
Lord of the universe
I surrender myself to you, thousands of times.
I quit being an artist.

ZIYABEG (BORN 1998)
TRANSLATED BY AZIZ ISA ELKUN

A STRING OF DEWDROPS

Good words can drip from soul to soul
They give vibrant colours to the flowers
They are sweetest when strung together
But who will pluck a melody from them?

Words
Written by the poet who can read minds
And pages that are from his isolated heart.

Without ink
Poems would be written on the surface of the earth
Humans and love were created at the very beginning
From or between words, eyes, and hearts.

TRANSLATED BY AZIZ ISA ELKUN

I LOST MYSELF

Photos of dogs and cats
Put inside lovely frames
They hang them everywhere
Declaring 'my beloved pet is lost'.

People search for their dog or cat
When they go missing
However, I am lost myself
And no one has searched for me.

I have been lost for such a long time
It has probably been a few centuries
But no missing person poster was put anywhere
Nor did anyone pay attention.

I have no father or mother, nor siblings
No one loves or cares for me
I am tiring of searching for myself
There is no trace of where I have been.

Have I disappeared in the darkness?
Have I been exhausted by endless suffering?
Like the river that disappeared from my homeland
Have I been erased from the souls of my people?

TURSUNGUL ABDULLAH (BORN 1963)
TRANSLATED BY AZIZ ISA ELKUN

SHARING MY SORROW

When I tell my sorrows to the Moon at night
It quietly hides behind the clouds
And when I share my grief with the stars
They close their eyes while they sparkle.

When I share my grievance with a path
It suddenly disappears before my eyes
Sorrow pierces my heart and makes me uneasy
Because I am not even able to walk freely.

Separation looms like a tall tower
Has anyone else fallen in love along these paths?
Shedding tears and suffering for a lover
My love is grieving, her hunched posture is a ridge.

All I long for is to drink the wine of love
But I fear that moment will not come soon
My poor heart is sorely oppressed
My weary soul, why does the sun hide?

28 September 2018

230   ABDIKHEYIR KHELIL TAWAKKUL (BORN 1984)
TRANSLATED BY AZIZ ISA ELKUN

THE RAIN, YOU AND ME

I am going to push you away as you try to reach
    my soul
Through joining the raindrops.
The raindrops that shine under streetlamps
Become pearls on the window.
I found myself seeking your eyes among the stars
And I tightly closed my own.
I tried to pretend not to see your shadow
On the road while you wandered around.
My eyes are now dim, and all is a blur
I glare at the rainy wind that carries your scent.
My thoughts have left, searching for you
I have expelled them to a distant place
None of them will be able to return, until you
    return to me.

SOLITUDE

A bird which does not have room in its nest
Commits suicide, hanging from a branch of a tree.

The last tear shed for love
Lies unconscious on the petals of a red rose.

Death was hastening to a mourning ceremony
And on the shore a suffering fish lay in the sun.

The stages of fate are fascinating
It is more complicated than you think.

GRIEVANCE

You are a forgotten spirit
That once smiled on the lips of a colourful flower.

You are a story of comfort told by a grieving mother
Engraved in her memory.

You are the consciousness of the Taklimakan*
The echo of prehistoric travellers.

* The Taklimakan is the second largest shifting sand desert in
the world, located in south-western Uyghuristan.

ABDUWELI TURSUN (BORN 1970)
TRANSLATED BY AZIZ ISA ELKUN

NOTHING

They say that time can heal anything
And that regret causes agony
They say that faithfulness is everything
Yet I still cannot earn your love.

One day you may forget the pain of separation
You may no longer desire to see your loved one
No longer desire to see the flame burning in his eyes
But I can't erase your eyes from my heart.

They say that we humans can get used to anything
They say that you burn like a haystack for a while
And then you fall in love with another beauty
But I can't detach you from my soul.

They say that if you open your eyes opportunities
    will come
I hope one day soon this ordeal will pass
There will be new love
And joy will return
But I am powerless to remove you from my heart.

2 June 2017

BLOCKED EMOTIONS

Quiet and solitary under the night sky,
Swimming alone towards the limitless universe,
Seeking my soulmate amongst the stars,
I felt my heart seared by the birth of hope.

Embarrassed, I met with the moon,
The moon girl greeted me, 'Salam,' she said.
Had she seen my melancholy heart?
Gently smiling she said, 'Shall we talk?'

'At last we have managed to meet,
My guest from the ancient Tarim basin,
Are you still alive under my light?
Is the Taklimakan desert still sleeping?'

My blocked emotions returned to me,
I left the moon girl's questions unanswered.
Bitter pain piercing my heart,
I left her, eyes cast down in the twilight.

Aqsu, 12 December 1998

WRITTEN AND TRANSLATED BY
AZIZ ISA ELKUN (BORN 1970)

I ASK IF MY SPRING HAS ARRIVED

When in the morning the spring bird sings,
When the garden is full of spring scent
And the breeze kisses my chin and flees,
I ask if my spring has arrived.

Elkun is thinking of the distant past
Desiring every long-awaited spring
Wishing for an end to dark winter
I ask if my spring has arrived.

Though rain falls like the tears of the grief-stricken,
Though there may be thunderstorms,
Though there is dew or frost on the flowers,
I ask if my spring has arrived.

Though the cranes fly in a long line across the sky,
Though the swans have returned and found their
    nests,
Though the lambs lap at the snowmelt,
I ask if my spring has arrived.

Though the poplar flowers are dropping to the
    ground,
Though the cuckoo's call is heard by its mate,
Though our girls pick henna from the fields,
I ask if my spring has arrived.

The farmers' desires are fulfilled by the land
They praise the spring singing a Nowruz song*
Children look towards the green horizon
I ask if my spring has arrived.

When the dew forms in spring,
When the apricot and willow blossoms fall,
When my grandmother's wheat ears sprout in the
    gourd,
I ask if my spring has arrived.

Elkun's heart cannot smile any more
Because winter has not yet gone from the farmer's
    home,
So he calls the spring with ardent love,
I ask you, please come, my spring!

London, 12 February 2016

* Nowruz, the first day of spring, or the beginning of a new
year based on the Iranian Solar Hijri calendar. The Nowruz
festival, held on 21 March, is popular among Persian and
Turkic peoples. Uyghurs gather together, make Nowruz dishes,
play traditional games such as horse and camel racing, tug of
war, or wheel spinning, and write poems about the changing
seasons. Reading poetry (*Mushaira*) is an important part of the
Nowruz celebration, a chance to voice the innermost thoughts,
feelings and desires of the Uyghur people. Sadly, neither
Nowruz nor Uyghur poetry can be freely celebrated in the
Uyghur homeland today.

THE SPRING BIRD

Adding to my early morning mood
A bird sings to herald the spring
Pink-white apricot blossoms flower
My heart misses my lover.

Timid bird on the white blossom branches
Sing your joyful song of life
Petals reflecting bright sunlight
Flutter a greeting to the teasing breeze.

White blossom, like a bridal gown
If I were a spring bird perched on your branch
I would sink into your petals with no regret
And serenade you at dawn and dusk.

Sing, bird of freedom, never cease your song
The time has come to summon the spring
Banish dark winter from our garden
It is the season to sing to your lover.

These sweet feelings warm my soul
And link me to mother nature
Every spring I sprout like a sapling
My poems will grow like trees.

16 March 2016

HOPES FLOAT ON THE MEDITERRANEAN

The sun shines above the volcano
By the sea where Mussolini's boot burned*
Their green orchards were full of fruit
Their fortresses were the tallest of all.

Fish swim merrily through the teeming sea
The smell of wine has yet to vanish from the pot
A couple on the beach forget about the world
A love song sung at high tide.

The silver-coated water shimmers
Lovers' sailing boats blush on the horizon
Under that unlucky mountain with sorrow in its heart
That erupted and made the earth tremble.

Lovers' tragic stories are carried by the boats
On this island countless babies were born
Yet how many hopes were drowned in the sea
Tears fall from dark clouds onto the earth's face.

The cathedral's towers stand in rebellion
The god of love is sunk deep in silence
These ancient fortresses were left to us by kings
They do not flinch from telling us the truth.

The colourful street leads straight to the fortress
Every step reminds me of Kashgar
The noodles and pastries here are just like our own
The figs of Atush grow here all year round.

Hopes are floating on the Mediterranean Sea
They arouse great desire in this desert boy's heart
Gusts of wind kiss my chin unasked
They drag me down to the sea to swim with the sun.

This island has witnessed countless ages
The spirit of the Romans has become a legend
Elkun seeks a moment of comfort here
Even though his life belongs to the Tarim.

Cagliari, Sardinia, Italy, 20 September 2016

* The Uyghur revolutionary poet Lutpulla Mutellip, who
was executed in 1945, wrote a famous shorty story in 1943
expressing his stance against fascism. In 'The Last Fight for
Survival' he describes the Italian peninsula as Mussolini's boot
and says, 'Mussolini's boot is burning in the Mediterranean
Sea.' Since then, Mussolini's regime is always depicted in
Uyghur literature as a 'burning boot' and the term is used as
an anti-war slogan.

FATHER
An Obituary

Dedicated to my beloved father who left us on 3 November 2017. Rest in peace.

A bright star stopped shining in the garden of life
angels read verses to send him to Heaven
Elkun, your only son who failed to carry your coffin
says 'my dear father' and pens this eulogy . . .

When the leaves of the white poplar trees that you
    planted
fall this autumn you won't be here
and when the grapes ripen on the vine
you won't be here to eat them.

Sheep bleat for you from their enclosure
your hard-working hands are not there to feed them
even the roosters fall silent to mourn you at dawn
now you are not here, your house lacks its pillar.

My sky is covered with heavy dark clouds
the sun I awaited did not rise today
you were the moon who lit my soul
now day has become night without you.

In our village you were known as a gardener
you won't be there when the desert blooms through
    your labour
when your grandchild sets out on the sea of
    knowledge
when she calls 'grandfather' you won't be there.

Dear father, you were a gardener with green fingers
now when the thorns grow, you won't be there to
    prune them
you were a doctor, and to your patients you were an
    angel
now my heart is broken but you are not here to cure it.

You have left today in your coffin heading towards
    your tomb
because he was not beside you when you died, your
    son did not carry you
when seven spades of soil were dropped upon you
everyone bade you farewell but I was not there.

My soul is burning fiercely with this loss
let Elkun cry now for he has his father no more
I couldn't see you alive for one last time . . .
how sad I am and can find no cure for my grief.

London, 8 November 2017

CHIMENQUSH – A FLOWER BIRD

This poem is dedicated to Chimengül Awut. Chimengül is a
well-known Uyghur poet whose pen name is 'Chimenqush'
(a flower bird). She worked as a senior editor for the
Kashgar Uyghur Publishing House before being sent to
China's 'Re-education Camps' in July 2018.

Chimenqush
The flower bird of Kashgar
The moment before the smell of hot summer went
    away
You were happy singing in the village
Your footprints were still fresh in the dust.

So I said:
I can't believe you have become a wilted flower
I can't believe you have become a caged bird
I want to break the lock of that cage
I want to curse all the locks in our world
I want to burn away all evil with my rage
The fire of revenge will consume it . . .

Your poems will soar
In the blue sky where you belong
Because the sky is free, unlike you
It can visit you through your narrow window
When you feel sad . . .

Chimenqush
I know you were never afraid of the seasons
I know no one can cheat you
You will return one day
You will come back next spring
Holding a bunch of flowers in your hand.

If you do not come
The poplar trees will not blossom
The peach trees will not bloom in Beshkerem*
Swallows will not fly over the city of Kashgar
Life will not go on without you!

London, 1 November 2018

* Beshkerem – a small town near Kashgar city, famous for its
peaches.

BORDERS

Borders
How long
Have you been a source of conflict?
You did not exist
At the time of Adam and Eve
When they learned how to love.

Why did humans create you?
Why are they obsessed with you?
Why are there so many wars because of you?

No border, no power has the right
To take away what was given by God.

We were born to live free
I am ashamed to see humans caged behind walls.

I want to break this iron cage
I want to break the world's silence
I want to fly
Free as a bird in the blue sky.

15 February 2019

'YOU DID NOT RETURN . . .'

My mother said:
'You will come back
When the apricot trees start to blossom
When the birds sing their spring songs
But you didn't come back
Instead, all the swallows have returned . . .'

My father said:
'You will come back
When autumn leaves fall . . .'

But demons didn't wait until that day.

In the end, it was he who fell
My father turned into the leaves
My angel has disappeared.

And still, I have not returned.

25 March 2019

CLOUDS HID THE MOON

Much larger than myself
My longing is growing like a poplar tree
Exhausted from waiting on the shore of love
It curses our separation in a language
No one ever heard before.

Every night I slept in fear
But on that night when clouds hid the Moon
The words of my grandfather echoed in my ears
And I remembered myself and set off
To discover freedom
In a faraway land where the horizon lies
Although it is far away from my love.

On this journey of life
There are many invisible obstacles
And a devil hides in the bright Moon.

I gazed at the shining stars
And one blinked back at me
On that night, when I was playing hide-and-seek with
    my friends
The same Moon was hidden behind clouds
And I made a promise to myself –
I would never abandon my dreams.

I detested the fate that was designed for me
My mother said it was given before I was born
And was written on my brow so only fairies could
    read it.

Now I write poetry
Now I write an obituary for bad luck
Wishing it would go away and never return
For the Uyghurs, whom a devil cursed with ill
     fortune.

My regret stretches out beyond the window
And my two fates are reflected in the glass
On one side profound dejection,
A lingering residue from the past
On the other, a resilient spirit ignites in defiant hope.

I am flying, riding my dreams
My love is calling me in a desperate voice
Saying, 'Do not come back after the gates of hell
     close.'

I can see cranes flying in the night sky
The full moon's glow illuminates the clouds
I am still recovering
From fierce battles between sorrow and hope
On that starless night you perished
When clouds hid the melancholic Moon.

14 December 2021

ROSES

Dedicated to my mother and to all innocent Uyghurs who have beeen arrested and detained in China's twenty-first-century concentration camps since 2017.

It's a morning bright with sun
Another new day has started
I count, altogether twenty-two autumns
And winters have passed in exile
And I don't know how many years remain
Until I can return to the place where I belong
To the land that my forefathers made home

I can feel the sorrow in myself
My soul shivers; it's cold
I inherited this sorrow from my father
Whenever the memory of my vanished homeland
Returns and occupies my mind
It inspires me to be human with dignity
Able to call for the survival of a lost nation
Able to appeal for mercy and love
From the world
Again and again

The place where I was born
Has turned into a heap of ghostly relics
It exists only as a memory
In this world full of selfishness

I am sitting in a garden chair
Trying to enjoy, for a minute, the warm sun
But it is quickly covered by the scudding clouds
A steaming cup of coffee evaporates my gloom
I am still struggling to feel myself
Believing that after tomorrow better days will come
One day life will smile on us
Even on the man who writes these lines
Although he lost everything
Travelling on the road of no return
And lived a second life
He is still a hostage to that place
He lives with constant fear

The monster has left countless scars
It has pierced me with needles
But still I call for justice for those
Who have suffered more
But my spirit is still fighting
My hope is still alive
Each time I find new courage
It brings the joy of a smile

Although it's autumn
The leaves in my garden are still green
The first rose I planted three years ago
To mark the destruction of my father's grave
The second rose I planted
On Mothers' Day last year
The third rose I planted for the unknown Uyghurs
Who survive inside the camps

My roses are blossoming with hope
Singing a song of freedom
Without waiting for the spring
They remind us
How beautiful it is to be alive
To live in peace in our beautiful world.

London, 10 October 2021

BIOGRAPHIES
(Modern and Contemporary poets)

MAHMUD KASHGARI (pp. 27–33), a renowned Uyghur
scholar, was born in 1005 CE in Kashgar, the capital city
of the Qarakhanid Empire. He adopted the pen name
Kashgari, derived from his birthplace. Kashgari served
as a scholar at the palace of the Qarakhanid rulers
and travelled extensively across Central Asia. During
his journeys, spanning many years, he meticulously
documented his observations and insights, which
culminated in his famous *Diwan-i Lughat al-Turk*
(also known as *Turki Tillar Diwani*, and in English as
Compendium of the Turkic Dialects), completed between
1072 and 1074. This monumental work is not only an
important source in Turkic linguistics, but also provides
a comprehensive account of Turkic and Uyghur customs
and folklore, epics and rhymes, history and geography.
Notably, Kashgari holds the distinction of being the
first person to draw a map of the world that includes an
accurate depiction of Japan. Dedicating his work to the
Abbasid Caliph in Baghdad, he introduced the Turkic
languages, customs and traditions to the Arabic world,
making a landmark contribution to cross-cultural
exchange. Kashgari died in 1102 at the age of ninety-
seven. He continues to be held in great esteem by
Uyghurs and throughout the Turkic world, and his tomb
on Mount Upal, near Kashgar, has become a pilgrimage
site.

YUSUF HAS HAJIB BALASAGHUNI (pp. 34–9) (*c*.1019–85) was born in the city of Balasaghun, the capital of the Qarakhanid Empire, and later moved to Kashgar, where he completed the *Kutadgu Bilig.*

KHOJA AHMAD YASAWI (pp. 40–44), a great Sufi poet and sheikh, is believed to have been born in the twelfth century in Sayram, a town in present-day Kazakhstan. He is well known as the founder of the Yasawiyya Sufi order. He is the earliest poet named as an author of verses in the Uyghur Muqam musical repertoire.

ALI-SHIR NAVA'I (pp. 45–58) was an important figure in the fifteenth-century Timurid court in Herat, and a major poet in the Central Asian tradition, celebrated as a cultural icon by Uyghurs and Uzbeks. His lyrics are often sung within the Uyghur Twelve Muqam tradition. His works mark a watershed in the history of Turkic-language poetry, and he is known as the founder of the Chagatay literary language. Born in 1441 in Herat, Nava'i was the descendant of Uyghur bakshi scholars employed by the Timurid royal family, and a follower of the Naqshbandi Sufi order. He acquired great personal wealth, and served as a high official in the Timurid court until his death in 1501. The well-known love poem on p. 45 features – in a contemporary Uyghur-language version – in the first (Chebiyat) Muqam, performed as part of the Uyghur Twelve Muqam musical suites. (Roughly 20%–30% of the Muqam song lyrics are extracted from Nava'i's poems.)

ZAHIR-UD-DIN MUHAMMAD BABUR (pp. 59–64), founder
of the Mughal Empire, was born on 14 February 1483
in Andijan (in modern Uzbekistan). His father was a
descendant of Timur; his mother, Kutluk Nigar, through
her father Yunas Khan, was a descendant of Genghis
Khan. Her nephew, Babur's cousin Said Khan, founded
the Saidiye Uyghur Kingdom in Yarkand (in modern
Uyghuristan) in 1514. Babur lost his own small Central
Asian principality while still a child, but eventually
carved out a new kingdom for himself in Afghanistan.
From there he began his invasions of India, where he
established the Mughal Empire though he himself ruled
for just four years, dying at Agra on 26 December 1530.
For all the wealth and power that his conquest brought
him, Babur remained homesick for his native country,
and many of his poems are about the pain of exile. The
famous *Baburnama* (Memoirs of Babur) was originally
written in the Chagatay Turkic (Uyghur) language. His
divan contains 118 ghazals and more than 200 rubaiyats.

BABA RAHIM MASHRAB (pp. 65–75) is one of the great
Chagatay-language poets of Central Asia, whose poems
and stories are strongly influenced by Sufi imagery and
ideals. He was born in the Andijan region of present-day
Uzbekistan in 1657 and grew up in the nearby town of
Namangan. When he was a teenager he went to Kashgar
to follow the Naqshbandi Sufi saint and religious leader
Afaq Khoja. He lived in Kashgar and Khotan and over
the decades travelled to many cities and towns in the
Uyghur homeland. While visiting Afghanistan in 1711,
he was accused of insulting religion and killed on the

orders of Mahmud Khan, Governor of Balkh. Since Mashrab's time in Kashgar his poems have been very popular among the Uyghurs, and many of them are still sung as part of the Uyghur Twelve Muqam musical suites.

MUHAMMAD SIDIQ ZELILI (p. 76) was a Uyghur Sufi poet and musician believed to have been born in 1676 in Yarkand, then the capital city of the Saidiye Uyghur Kingdom. He passed the greater part of his life under the subsequent Khoja dynasty (members of the Sufi Naqshbandi order), dying in Yarkand in 1755. At the age of nearly forty he embarked on a long pilgrimage through the desert, visiting the shrines of saints, about which he wrote in his travelogue, the *Safarnama*. He was the author of a divan, and the *Tezkire* [memoir] *of Khoja Muhammad Sherif Buzrukwar*. Many of his poems are sung in the Uyghur Twelve Muqam.

MUHAMMAD EMIN GHOJAMQULI GUMNAM (who also used the pen name Hirqiti) (p. 77) is one of the best-known Sufi poets of the Uyghurs. He was born in Tazghun, a small town near Kashgar, in 1633, and died in 1724. Gumnam studied for sixteen years at the famous Saidiye Madrassah in Kashgar. He and his father worked at the court of Hideytullah Afaq Khoja, the powerful saint and ruler of Kashgar. He wrote many epic poems (dastans), and two books, *Diwan-i Gumnam* and *Muhabbetname we Mehnetkam*. Some of his lyrics are still sung today in the Uyghur classical musical suites – the Uyghur Twelve Muqam.

MOLLA BILAL NAZIMI (p. 78) was born in Ghulja (a city in the north of the Uyghur region) in 1824. He was a well-known literary realist, whose most famous works are the epics *Nuzugum* and *Ghazat der Mulki Chin* and the lyric poems, *Ghezeliyat*. He also wrote numerous essays and articles on contemporary Uyghur issues. In his later years be became blind and lived in poverty, dying in Yarkent (in modern Kazakhstan) in 1900. This poem was written after the death of Nazimi's older brother Jalalidin. It is performed in the Uyghur Twelve Muqam repertoires.

ABDUHALIQ UYGHUR (pp. 91–3) is a well-known poet, born on 9 February 1901 into an intellectual and business family in the city of Turpan in Uyghuristan. In his twenties he travelled to the Soviet Union and Finland. He learned Russian and studied Russian literature for three years. After his return to Turpan, he began to write poems to raise awareness and call the Uyghurs to fight for their freedom. He was executed by a Chinese warlord in Turpan when he was thirty-two, on 13 March 1933.

LUTPULLA MUTELLIP (pp. 94–8), poet and journalist, is one of the most influential figures in modern Uyghur poetry. He was born on 22 November 1922 and executed by the Chinese police, aged twenty-two, on 18 September 1945 in the city of Aqsu. His poems were collected and published in the 1950s in Uyghur, Russian and Chinese. 'Answer to the Years' is regarded as one of his masterpieces.

QASIMJAN QEMBERI (pp. 99–101) was a poet and playwright. He was born in 1910 in the Boyamet town of Atush, and graduated from a Soviet Workers' school in Tashkent in 1927. After returning to his homeland in 1932, he worked for the Uyghur Sanayi Nefisiye organization which aimed to promote and revive Uyghur culture. His pen name was 'Inaq' (Unity). He brought many classic Uyghur plays to the stage and created modern Uyghur theatre culture in the 1940s. During the Second East Turkistan Republic from 1945 to 1949, he actively participated as a leader in the government. He passed away in Kashgar in 1956.

AHMED ZIYA'I (p. 102) was a prolific poet, playwright and journalist. He was born in Kashgar in 1913 and worked as an editor for the Kashgari newspaper *Yengi Hayat* (The New Life) from 1935 to 1949. He was frequently arrested and spent extensive time in prison. In 1980, after China's Cultural Revolution, he was invited to research Uyghur classic literature at the Xinjiang Social Science Academy. He passed away on 27 October 1989 in Urumchi.

NIMSHEHIT ARMY ELI SAYRAMI (pp. 103–4), a well-known modern poet, was born in Sayram, a town in Bay County, in 1904. He worked as a secretary for the First East Turkistan Republic in Kashgar in 1933. When the Chinese Dungan army attacked Kashgar, he fought in the front line. He was hit in the neck by a bullet and nearly died, earning the nickname 'Himshehit' (Half-martyr), which he adopted as his pen name. He was killed on 24 August 1971 by the Red Guards during China's Cultural Revolution.

MELIKE ZIYAWUDUN (pp. 105–6) was born in 1938 in Urumchi. She graduated from Beijing Art school in 1956, and worked as a presenter for the Xinjiang Song and Dance Ensemble. She wrote many poems. 'Séni esleymen' (I will remember you), became one of the most popular songs among the Uyghurs in the late 1970s and 1980s. Melike Ziyawudun was arrested by the Red Guards on 14 October 1969 because her grandfather, Khoja Niyaz Haji, was one of the leaders of the Uyghur independence movement. On 22 June 1970 she was killed in prison. Her later poems reflect the hardships experienced during the years of China's Cultural Revolution. Her lyrics are still popular with Uyghurs today; they serve as a reminder of those traumatic years of suffering, but they are also dedicated to love, compassion, and hope for a beautiful future.

ABDUREHIM ÖTKÜR (pp. 107–15), a prominent poet and writer, was born on 1 May 1923 in Qumul. His historical novels and poems in various styles are widely read. He started publishing his poems in the 1940s. Like many Uyghur intellectuals, Ötkür spent many years in jail during the Cultural Revolution. He passed away on 5 October 1995 in Urumchi.

DOLQUN YASIN (pp. 116–17), celebrated poet and journalist, was born in Korgas County in the Ili region in 1938. He migrated with his family to Soviet Kazakhstan, and then studied at Tashkent University. He began to publish his poetry in 1951. He passed away on 5 September 2005 in Almaty. He is one of the most celebrated Uyghur poets in Kazakhstan.

TURGHUN ALMAS (pp. 118–19), poet and historian, was born in Kashgar on 30 October 1924. He was jailed from 1943 to 1946 and again from 1947 to 1949 for his political activities. In 1950 he became editor of the *Azadliq* (Liberation) newspaper. Turghun Almas is best known for his historical book, *Uyghurlar* (The Uyghurs), which was banned by the Chinese authorities soon after its publication in 1992. Subsequently he was accused of 'supporting ethnic nationalism and separatism' and placed under house arrest in Urumchi. He passed away on 11 September 2001.

TÉYIPJAN ÉLIYOW (p. 123), well-known poet and journalist, was born in April 1930 in the Ili region of the Uyghur homeland. He worked as a writer for the newspaper of the short-lived Second East Turkistan Republic in 1945. He passed away in 1989.

MAHMUT ABDURAHMANOV (pp. 124–5), a respected poet, academic and musician, was born in 1934 in Tashkensaz County in the Almaty region of Kazakhstan, and graduated from Kazakh National University in 1958. He published many books and poetry collections. He passed away in February 2013 in Almaty.

AHMET IGAMBERDI (pp. 126–8) was a poet and journalist, born in Beshbaliq, near Urumchi, in 1937. He graduated from Tashkent State University in 1961, returning to Urumchi to work for *Miras* magazine as an editor. In 1985 he migrated to Australia with his family. He is one of the well-known exiled Uyghur poets.

ILYA BEKHTIYA (pp. 129–30) is a well-known poet from the Uyghur County of Soviet Kazakhstan, where he was born in 1932. He started publishing his poems in 1953 while studying literature at the Abay Teachers College in Almaty. He passed away in 1987.

MUHEMMETJAN RASHIDIN (pp. 131–4), who was born in Ghulja in 1940, is one of the most celebrated Uyghur poets. His poetic style is rhythmic, the language lively, and many of his poems have become song lyrics. He published several poetry collections, the first in 2001. He passed away on 13 November 2021 in Ghulja.

ABDUGHOPUR QUTLUQ (pp. 135–6) is a journalist, editor and poet. He was born in 1936 in Ghulja. During the border clash between the Soviet Union and China in 1962 he escaped to Kazakhstan, where he has published many poetry collections. He lives in Almaty.

ALMASBEK MEMTIMIN (pp. 137–8), well-known poet and critic – pen name 'Almasbek' – was born in Chochek city in the Uyghur homeland on 7 April 1943. He migrated with his parents to Soviet Kazakhstan in 1962, and graduated in journalism from Tashkent State University. His three volumes of poetry and essays are especially valued by Uyghur readers in Kazakhstan.

ZEYNURE ISA (pp. 139–41), poet, literary translator and academic, was born in Kashgar in 1941. She graduated from Urumchi University in 1965 and her first poetry collection was published in 1966. She migrated to Turkey in 1985. She is the author of many books and poems. She passed away in Istanbul on 8 January 2022.

KÜRESH KÖSEN (p. 142), a prominent composer, musician and poet, was born in 1959 in Urumchi. He worked as a teacher for the Xinjiang Arts Institute. In 1996 he fled to Turkey and through the UN went on to Sweden in 1999 as a political refugee. He passed away on 29 October 2006.

ABDUREHIM ABDULLAH (pp. 143–4) is a well-known writer, poet and scriptwriter, born in February 1955 in Kelpin County in the Aqsu region of Uyghuristan. He worked as an editor for Xinjiang Audio-Video publishing house. He has written many poems, stories and novels. His writing style is unique and densely metaphorical, and he is deeply interested in the lives of Uyghur people past and present. His essays explore the fate of his nation and seek justice and freedom for the Uyghurs. His poetry is popular, especially with singers, since many of them have been set to music. Abdurehim Abdullah was arrested in April 2017. Since then, there has been no news of his whereabouts.

NURMEMET YASIN ORKISHI (pp. 145–6) is an award-winning Uyghur writer born in the town of Awat in Maralbesh County in 1977. He is known for his numerous short stories, essays and three volumes of poetry: *First Love, Crying from the Heart* and *Come on Children*. His famous short story 'The Wild Pigeon' ('Yawa kepter') has been translated into English. After a closed trial in February 2005, Yasin was sentenced by the Maralbesh County Court to ten years in prison. Since then, there has been no news of his whereabouts.

OSMANJAN SAWUT (pp. 147–8), a poet and editor, was born in Manas County of Uyghuristan in 1945. He graduated from Urumchi University in 1961 with a degree in Uyghur literature. He is the author of many poems and essays. He passed away in October 2013 in Urumchi.

EKHMETJAN OSMAN (pp. 149–53) is a celebrated Uyghur poet born in Urumchi in 1964. He is the founder of a new poetry movement, the *gungga* (hazy) poems. He began studying Uyghur literature at Urumchi University in 1981, but the following year went to Syria to study at Damascus University. Since 2004 he has been living in Canada. One of his poetry collections was published in English in 2015 under the title *Uyghurland, the Farthest Exile.*

ABDUQADIR JALALIDIN (p. 154), who was born in 1964, is a renowned poet, scholar and professor of literature at Xinjiang Normal University, Urumchi. He was detained in April 2018 and has not been heard of since. His writings are popular, as are his literary translations into Uyghur, which include George Orwell's *Animal Farm.* He visited London for six months as a scholar in 2006.

PERHAT TURSUN (pp. 155–63), one of the most celebrated contemporary Uyghur poets and writers, was detained around January 2018. In February 2020 reports emerged that the Chinese authorities had sentenced him to sixteen years in prison. His current situation is unknown. Perhat Tursun is well known for his poetry and novels. He is the author of *One Hundred Love Lyrics,*

The Art of Suicide and *Messiah Desert*. He was awarded the Tucholsky Prize by Swedish PEN in September 2022.

ABLET ABDURISHIT BERQI (TARIM) (pp. 164–6) is a prominent poet and academic. He was born in Lop County, Khotan, in 1971. He was an associate professor at Xinjiang Institute of Education, and later conducted postdoctoral research at Haifa University (2014–16). Just before leaving Israel he sent his unpublished poetry by email to Aziz Isa Elkun. After his return home he was arrested and sentenced to thirteen years' imprisonment.

ADIL TUNYAZ (pp. 167–73) amazed the Uyghur world with his poem, written in 1992, 'Qeshqerdiki yershari' ('The World in the City of Kashgar'), and he became one of the most celebrated poets of the 1990s. He was born in 1970 into a teacher's family in Qaghiliq County in the Kashgar Prefecture. After graduating from the literature faculty of Urumchi University in 1993, he worked as a journalist for the Xinjiang People's Radio Station. According to media reports, Adil Tunyaz was arrested in December 2017. His whereabouts and fate are still unknown.

RAHIM YASIN QAYNAMI (pp. 174–5) was born in Khorgas County, Uyghuristan, in 1975. He began writing poetry in 1996 and his work has been published in magazines throughout the Uyghur region, where he is well known for his free-verse style. According to friends, he was arrested and taken to an internment camp at the beginning of 2018. Since then, there has been no information about him. Our thanks go to Muqaddes, from Japan, who has collected Qaynami's poems.

CHIMENGÜL AWUT (pp. 176–9) is a well-known Uyghur poet, who writes under the pen name 'Chimenqush' ('flower bird'). She was born in Kashgar on 6 December 1973. From 1996 she worked for the Kashgar Uyghur Publishing House as a senior editor before being sent to China's 'Re-education Camps' in July 2018.

GHOJIMUHEMMED MUHEMMED (pp. 180–83) was born in 1971 in Guma County in the Khotan Prefecture. He began publishing poetry in the 1990s, and his work has earned enormous respect from the Uyghur community. His unique poetic style revolts against the society he lived in. He passed away on 12 July 2018.

GÜLNISA IMIN GÜLKHAN (pp. 184–6) was born in November 1976 in Chira County in the Khotan Prefecture of Uyghuristan, and worked as a teacher for Chira County Second High School. She was detained and sent to the internment camps in December 2018, and in 2019 she was sentenced to seventeen years and six months' imprisonment on a charge of 'separatism' in her poetry. Gülnisa wrote more than a thousand poems, many of which were published in literary magazines; she provided a powerful voice of discontent and resistance in Uyghur society.

RISALET MERDAN (pp. 187–91), poet and literary translator, was born in the town of Tarati in the Qomul region in 1970. She began to publish her poetry in 1995. She works as a teacher in Chira County in the Khotan Prefecture.

MUYESSER ABDUL'EHED (HENDAN) (pp. 192–5),
celebrated woman poet, was born in 1984 in Ghulja
in the north of Uyghuristan, and is known by her pen
name, Hendan. She began to write poems and essays
while studying medicine at Peking University. After
migrating to Turkey in 2013, she founded Ayhan
Education, an organization devoted to fostering and
teaching the Uyghur language in the diaspora. Her
recent work grapples with the crisis in her homeland;
her debut novel, *Kheyr-khosh, quyash* (Farewell to the
Sun), is the first extended work of fiction to focus on the
detention camps. Hendan appears on the BBC's 2020 list
of 100 inspiring and influential women from around the
world. She currently lives in Istanbul.

ABDUSHUKUR MUHAMMET (pp. 196–9) was born in
Kucha County in 1967. He studied Uyghur literature at
the Kashgar Teachers College and worked in Urumchi as
a teacher before migrating to Sweden in 2003. He is the
author of many books, and a collection of his poetry was
published in Turkish in 2021.

OMER IMIN (pp. 200–201) was born in 1967 in Toqsu
County and graduated from Urumchi University in
1988. He left his hometown in 1996, and arrived in
Munich, Germany where he applied for political asylum.
He has lived there ever since. He published his first
poetry collection in 2016.

RAHILE KAMAL (pp. 202–3) is a poet and journalist.
She was born in the city of Ghulja city in 1968. She
graduated in journalism from Urumchi University in

1993 and worked as a journalist for the *Ili Kechlik Géziti* (Ili evening newspaper). Since 2004 she has been living in Sweden. Her first poetry collection, *Kamal Has Gone* was recently published (in Uyghur) in Turkey.

SABIRAM ANWAROVA (p. 204), poet and journalist, was born in 1998 in the Uyghur County of Kazakhstan. She graduated from the Teachers College of Kazakhstan. Since 2017 she has been working as a journalist for the *Voice of Uyghurs* state newspaper in Kazakhstan.

ABIDE ABBAS NESIRIDIN (p. 205) was born in Uyghuristan in 1992. Her poetry is known for its unique expressive style. She lives in Istanbul.

ABDUREHIM PARACH (p. 206) was born in 1974 in Peyziwat County, Kashgar, and studied at the Kashgar Teachers College. On 30 June 1997, on the eve of Hong Kong's return to China, Parach was one of a group of Uyghur students arrested on the grounds of 'separatism' and 'splitting the country' and sentenced to three years in prison without any legal process. This marked the beginning of many years of harassment, and in 2013 Parach secretly left home and began a long journey which took him through inner China, Burma, Thailand and Malaysia before arriving in Turkey in August 2014. Since then he has been completely cut off from his wife and five children. His collected poems, *The Melody of Homelessness*, was published in Turkey in 2018.

SUMEYYE HAMDULLAH AYTURK (pp. 207–8) was born in Urumchi in 2000. She is currently studying in Istanbul.

ALIMJAN METQASIM GHEMNAKI (pp. 209–10) was born in Khotan County in 1992. He has been living in Turkey since 2013. Many of his poems have been translated into Turkish and published in Turkey.

MERDAN EHET'ÉLI (pp. 211–12) was born in 1991 in the southern city of Khotan. He started writing poems in high school. He has translated Dickinson, Borges and other authors from Chinese into Uyghur. Since 2021 he has been living in France.

GÜLNAZ SAYDULLAYEVA (pp. 213–14) was born in the Uyghur County of Kazakhstan in 1980 and studied at Abay University in the department of Uyghur Studies. She started writing in childhood and became well known for her poetry and short stories, which have been published in Kazakhstan and other Central Asian countries.

TUYGHUN ABDUWELI (pp. 215–16) was born in Yurchi, a town in Kelpin County, in 1974. In 2004, he migrated to Canada. He is an active member of the Uyghur community within the diaspora.

ABDUWELI AYUP (pp. 217–19), poet and linguist, was born in Kashgar in 1973. After completing his studies at the University of Kansas in the US, he was arrested in Urumchi on 20 August 2013 and received an eighteen-month sentence for his involvement in setting up Uyghur-language schools in the region. He arrived in Turkey in August 2015. He gave a detailed interview on Al Jazeera News about how he was subjected to various tortures in a Chinese prison. Since July 2019 he has lived in Norway. He is a prominent human-rights activist in the Uyghur diaspora.

AYGUL ALIM (pp. 220–21) is also known to the Uyghurs by her pen name 'Tamche' – a dewdrop. She was born in Ghulja County in 1979. Themes of separation, love and missing the homeland run through many of her poems, which reflect the Uyghurs' lives in the diaspora. Since 2008, she has been living in Australia.

IHSAN ISMAYIL (UMUN) (pp. 222–3) was born in Ghulja in 1994. He went to Turkey in 2014 to study sociology and graduated in 2019. After that he worked as a stringer reporter for the Radio Free Asia Uyghur Service. Since May 2022 he has been living in Paris. His pen name, 'Umun', is an old Uyghur word meaning 'hope' or 'desire'.

MUSTAFA KHELIL DEWRAN (p. 224) was born in Kelpin County in 1986. He left home in 2011 and went to the Netherlands. He now lives in London.

VILYAM MOLUT (p. 225) was born in 1974 in the Uyghur County of Kazakhstan, and he works as a teacher at the Uyghur school in Almaty. In 1999 his poetry collection, *The Heavens of My Soul*, was published in Almaty. Since 2017 he has been chair of the Uyghur Youth Writers' Society, known as 'Waris'.

ABDULKHABER QADIR ERKAN (p. 226) was born in Khotan in 1990. Now, he lives in Turkey and is studying Turkish literature.

ZIYABEG (pp. 227–8) was born in Aqsu in 1998. Since 2015 he has been living in Turkey.

TURSUNGUL ABDULLAH (pen name TENHA ARAL) (p. 229) was born in Kucha County in 1963. She graduated from the Nationalities University of Beijing in 1984 with a degree in modern Uyghur language. Since 1999 she has been living in Australia.

ABDIKHEYIR KHELIL TAWAKKUL (p. 230) was born in Khotan in 1984. Since 2014 he has been living in Istanbul.

AYSIMANGUL YASIN OGHUZAY (p. 231) was born in Qaghliq County in 1997. She began writing poetry in 2015. She is now studying at a university in Istanbul.

ABDUWELI TURSUN (p. 232–3) was born in Tekes County in 1970. He began to publish his poetry in 1986. Since 2012 he has been living in Germany.

DILMURAT ABDUQEYUM (p. 234) was born in Kashgar in 1977. He graduated from Urumchi University and currently lives in Istanbul.

AZIZ ISA ELKUN (pp. 235–51), poet and academic, was born in Uyghuristan in 1970. He grew up in Shahyar County, close to the Tarim River on the northern edge of Taklimakan Desert. After graduating from Urumchi University in 1991, he was harassed and persecuted by the Chinese authorities because of his political activities as a student. He left home in the spring of 1999 and arrived in the UK as a political refugee in 2001. In 2009 he graduated from Birkbeck, University of London. He has published many poems and research articles in both Uyghur and English. He is an active member of the Uyghur Community and founder of the London Uyghur Ensemble. He worked for many years as secretary of the International PEN Uyghur Centre. He has also worked as a research affiliate on British Academy projects based at SOAS, University of London. He is a member of English PEN.

ACKNOWLEDGMENTS

Everyman's Library is grateful to the following copyright holders for permission to reproduce the poems and translations in this book.

MICHAEL R. BURCH for translations of 'My Feelings' by Yasin Dolqun and 'Traces' by Abdurehim Ötkür.

DENNIS DALY for 13 poems from *Twenty-One Ghazals* by Alisher Navoiy, translated from the Uzbek by Dennis Daly, Červená Barva Press, 2016. Copyright © 2016 by Dennis Daly.

JOSHUA L. FREEMAN for the following translations: 'Uyghur Impressions' and 'My Love' by Ekhmetjan Osman, *Sinoturcica*, 2011; 'Elegy' and 'Morning Feeling' by Perhat Tursun, *Hayden's Ferry Review* 48, 2011; 'Colorful Words' and 'History', *Harvard Review Online*, March 2017; 'Chronicle of an Execution', *Words Without Borders*, March 2016; 'I Opened My Door', *FWJ Plus*, Fall 2016; 'He Was Taken Away' by Muyesser Abdul'ehed Hendan, *NYR Daily*, 13 August 2020; 'Common Night' by Merdan Ehet'éli, *Asymptote*, October 2015. Revised translations of all ten poems copyright © 2023 by Joshua L. Freeman. Reprinted by permission.

NICHOLAS KONTOVAS for 'Neverending Song' by Téyipjan Éliyow; 'The Struggle Will Not Die' by Küresh Kösen; 'I Call Forth Spring' and 'Waste You Traitors, Waste' by Abdurehim Ötkür; and 'Long Live' by Muhemmet-jan Rashidin, from *Uyghur Poetry Reader for Students*, translated with notes by Nicholas Kontovas and edited by Gülnisa Nazarova (published by the Department of Central Eurasian Studies, Indiana University Bloomington, Bloomington, Indiana, USA).

NATHAN LIGHT and Lit Verlag for 18-line extract ('Know that Muhammad's essence was Arab . . .') from *Dīvān-i hikmat* by Khoja Ahmed Yasawi, taken from *Intimate Heritage: Creating Uyghur Muqam Song in Xinjiang* (published by Transaction Publishers, copyright © LIT VERLAG, Dr W. Hopf, Berlin, 2008.

JEFFREY YANG and DOLKUN KAMBERI for 'Three Poetry Fragments Unearthed at Turpan Bezeklik'; four poems from the *Diwan Lughat al-Turk* (from 'On Guests' and 'On Festivals'); two poems from 'On Knowledge' ('Gold is only ore . . .' and 'If there are no scholars . . .') by Yusuf Hajib Balasa-ghuni; and 'I Am Not a White Flag' by Abdurehim Ötkür from *Some Kind of Beautiful Signal*, coedited by Natasha Wimmer and Jeffrey Yang (Two Lines Press, Center for the Art of Translation, California, 2011), translation copyright © 2011 by Jeffrey Yang and Dolkun Kamberi. Used with permission from the translators.

University of Chicago Press for the excerpt from *Wisdom of Royal Glory* (Kutadgu Bilig): *A Turko-Islamic Mirror for Princes* by Yusuf Khass Hajib, translated by Robert Dankoff (Publications of the Center for Middle Eastern Studies, no. 16, University of Chicago Press, 1983).

ALSHER KHALILOV, director of MIR Publishers, Almaty, Kazakhstan for poems by Ilya Bekhtiya from Uyghur PEN Club, *Hemmidin weten ela*, edited by Rabik Ismaylov, MIR Publishers, Almaty, 2014 and poems by Mahmut Abdurahmanov and Dolqun Yasin from *Shi'eriyet Gulzari – Tallanma* (Poetry Garden – Collection), edited by Selimakhun Zaynalov, MIR Publishers, Almaty, 2007.

ABDUJELIL TURAN, director of Taklamakan Uyghur Publishing House, Istanbul, Turkey for poems from Zeynure Isa: *Tarim Qizi* (A Daughter of the Tarim), Taklamakan Uyghur Publishing House, Istanbul, 2008.

ABDUSHUKUR MUHAMMED, President of the World Uyghur Writers' Union for poems from *The Voiceless Birds*, World Uyghur Writers' Union, by

Tursungul Abdullah, Dilmurat Abduqeyum, Hamdullah Ayturk, Mustafa Khelil Dewran, Abdulkhaber Qadir Erkan, Alimjan Metqasim Ghemnaki, Omer Imin, Ihsan Ismayil, Rahile Kamal, Abide Abbas Nesiridin, Aysimangul Yasin Oghuzay, Abdurehim Parach, Abdikheyir Khelil Tawakkul, Abduweli Tursun, Ziyabeg.

The poets Muyesser Abdul'ehed (Hendan), Tuyghun Abduweli, Aygul Alim, Almasbek, Sabiram Anwarova, Abduweli Ayup, Merdan Ehet'éli, Ahmet Igamberdi, Vilyam Molut, Abdushukur Muhammet, Ekhmetjan Osman, Abdughopur Qutluq and Gülnaz Saydullayeva.

The translators Munawwar Abdulla and Ajinur Setiwaldi.

We are unable for obvious reasons to contact publishers and poets or their relatives in the Uyghur homeland. We acknowledge with thanks the use of poems by the following:

Abdurehim Abdullah; Turghan Almas; Chimengül Awut; Ablet Abdurishit Berqi; Téyipjan Éliyow; Gülnisa Imin Gülkan; Abduqadir Jalalidin; Risalet Merdan; Ghojimuhemmed Muhemmed; Nurmemet Yasin Orkishi; Abdurehim Ötkür from his poetry collection *Ömür menzillir* (The Journey of Life), Xinjiang People's Publishing House, Urumchi, 2008; Rahim Yasin Qaynami; Qasimjan Qemberi; Muhammetjan Rashidin from his poetry collection *Ana Taghlar* (Mountains of Mother), Xinjiang People's Publishing House, Urumchi, 2008; Osmanjan Sawut from his poetry collection *Zémin Qesidisi* (Elegy to the Earth), Xinjiang People's Publishing House, Urumchi, 2008; Nimshehit Army Eli Sayrami; Adil Tunyaz; Perhat Tursun from his poetry collection *Muhabbet lirikilliridin 100 parche* (One Hundred Love Lyrics), Xinjiang People's Publishing House, 1998 and online sources; Ahmed Ziya'i from *Essay Collections of Ahmed Ziya'i*, Xinjiang People's Publishing House, Urumchi, 1987; Melike Ziyawudun.

272